Nasser Kurdy, David Tucker

A Reply to Hate: Forgivin'

ANALYZING POLITICAL VIOLENCE

Edited by Bethan Johnson and John Richardson

1   *Nasser Kurdy, David Tucker*
     A Reply to Hate: Forgiving My Attacker
     ISBN 978-3-8382-1558-7

Nasser Kurdy, David Tucker

A REPLY TO HATE: FORGIVING MY ATTACKER

ibidem
Verlag

Bibliografische Information der Deutschen Nationalbibliothek
Die Deutsche Nationalbibliothek verzeichnet diese Publikation in der Deutschen
Nationalbibliografie; detaillierte bibliografische Daten sind im Internet über
http://dnb.d-nb.de abrufbar.

Bibliographic information published by the Deutsche Nationalbibliothek
Die Deutsche Nationalbibliothek lists this publication in the Deutsche Nationalbibliografie; detailed
bibliographic data are available in the Internet at http://dnb.d-nb.de.

ISBN-13: 978-3-8382-1558-7
© *ibidem*-Verlag, Stuttgart 2021
Alle Rechte vorbehalten

Printed in the EU

Table of Contents

Foreword

David Tucker

I first met Dr Nasser Kurdy in February 2019, where myself, Matthew Feldman and Amjid Khazir, the three of us representing Academic Consulting Services Ltd. (www.aca demicconsulting.co.uk), The Centre for Analysis of the Radical Right (www.radicalrightanalysis.com) and Media Cultured (www.mediacultured.org), had collaborated with Shazia Awan of Manchester City Council on a counter-extremism event for school pupils which was hosted by Manchester Metropolitan University. At the event, experts spoke on prejudice, extremism and violence, and there were two survivors of extremist violence discussing their experiences. One was Ahmad Nawaz, who on 16 December 2014 in Peshawar, Pakistan, was shot by the Taliban in an attack on his school; 150 students were brutally massacred that day along with teachers and educationalists. Amongst those murdered was Ahmad's brother, Harris. Ahmad survived the attack and has since become an ambassador for education and peace working across the world. The other invited speaker was Dr Nasser Kurdy. On Sunday 24 September 2017 Dr Kurdy was stabbed in his neck as he was entering his local Islamic Centre in Altrincham, Greater Manchester. Dr Kurdy did not see the attacker coming, and he has only been able to speculate as to why he was the victim of this sudden, awful, and life-altering split-second attack. Nevertheless, through all the physical pain, the confusion and at times fear engendered by this attack, Dr Kurdy managed to come through it in just a matter of hours and profess his forgiveness of his attacker. Further on in the book Dr Kurdy discusses how he has thought about distinguishing between the forgiveness of an attacker and the forgiveness of an attack itself. For now, it suffices to say that it is very much this reflectiveness that comes through when meeting Dr Kurdy, a thoughtfulness always combined with good humour and kindness, a personality that has been brought to bear on the more impersonal abstracts of crude violence. It is of relevance throughout that, in telling contrast to his kitchen-knife-wielding attacker, Dr Kurdy is a surgeon. He brings his medical expertise to bear in fascinating ways on his own injury and in thinking about the implications his analysis has, or could have, for a criminal investigation and trial. In a sense, this book is a story of two users of knives, and the contrast between how the two deploy their respective tools tells us something about extremist violence and possible responses to it.

Dr Kurdy has been telling the story of his attack and forgiveness to many different audiences since, and by 2019 had started to think about setting it down on the page, so we discussed what such a project might look like. For one thing, Dr Kurdy is very busy as an orthopaedic surgeon, and he did not feel he could simply write the book himself. We decided, therefore, to conduct interviews, with the intention being that much of the book would be told in the first person, in Dr Kurdy's voice, as well as I could capture and edit it for the page. Chapters 1 to 10 are derived from this methodology; they are Dr Kurdy's voice, as spoken in interview, then transcribed and edited, with the interviewer's voice removed along the way. However, we also wanted to include some more discursive work, some evidence of the conversational way in which much of the book had come about. To that end, Chapter 11 retains its interview format in order that the wider-ranging and reflective discussion therein, which looks back on the events of the preceding chapters, explores current projects Dr Kurdy is engaged in and looks forward, could be presented in a way closer to how it came about.

Towards the end of the book are shorter contributing texts by other people also affected by the attack. Family, friends and colleagues lay out how events had both short-term and longer-term effects on themselves as well as on the protagonist. These contributions set out multifarious manifestations of what Dr Kurdy has come to call in recent work with prison inmates a "ripple" effect, referring to the ramifications across a range of people that a single traumatic event will inevitably have. It is often a cliché to say that an attack is an attack on a particular "community", especially if such an act might very well be intended as precisely just such a synecdoche. But it is not only a British Muslim community in general that these interspersed voices speak for, but also for the personal, familial and multi-faith community close to the person at the centre of these events.

Dr Kurdy always wanted the concept of forgiveness to be at the centre, the heart, of this book. In this very intention he even perhaps unknowingly spoke about his thinking of, his hopes for, other people. The book is less a record of events for Dr Kurdy to retain as memory might fade, times change, as priorities and focuses shift. I believe, though it has never been articulated as such throughout the process of producing this book, that the hope can be that the events surrounding this particular act of extreme violence might bring about some good, whether that is in speaking to others in comparable circumstances, or in filling out the academic records, for those producing policy as much as for those producing research, of what can happen following such an act. Personally speaking, it has been inspiring to see how an act of hate has been turned to good in such a way as described in the chapters that follow.

Chapter 1

About Me

I would like to begin this book at my own beginnings. I was born in 1959 in Aleppo, Syria, which is also where my mother came from. Given my name and my Middle Eastern looks, it can surprise people to learn that my mother's maiden name is Gilbert Manjaka. It is a Christian name, and her surname is not Arabic. My uncles' first names are Tony and George, and my grandmother's name is Margaret, all from my mother's side of the family, the Christians of Aleppo. They have lived in Aleppo for generations. I remember when my uncle George was married in a church service in Aleppo and I was probably just seven or eight years old, walking alongside my brother as we carried candles down the aisle.

My father's side of the family is Muslim, and then on that side my grandfather is of Kurdish origin, hence the name Kurdy, and my grandmother is Circassian. Her origin is the Caucasus, a region between the Black Sea and the Caspian Sea north of Turkey. Sadly, the late nineteenth century witnessed a Circassian genocide with many forced to migrate south, some as far as Syria where my grandmother's family eventually settled. I know very little about my father's family other than they lived in Damascus in the well-known Kurdish district of Rukn al-Din where he was born. I have only little recollection of my early childhood and I don't recall my father mentioning much about his life when we lived in Damascus. I later found out that he had worked in the security services in Damascus and all over Syria. In 1966, when I was just seven years old, he had to flee Damascus after a coup, led by Nour el Din Atassi. There were personal conflicts between Atassi and our father and when Atassi became president our father had to make a swift exit to Jordan. He was helped greatly by his friends in Jordan and eventually he managed to gain Jordanian citizenship. This is why I tell my friends I am half Syrian, half Jordanian.

Looking at my father's photos from the 1950s, I am not surprised why my mother fell head over heels for him. He was tall and handsome, he was a good swimmer, and he had a presence. As might be imagined, my parents marrying was part of a somewhat difficult story because they went against usual traditions at the time of Muslims marrying Muslims and Christians marrying Christians. I met one of my Christian cousins a few years ago and they told me about the impact the marriage had on the community at the time, but my mother was going to have it her way and that was that. She did finish high school, which was exceptional in the 1950s, but beyond that she was self-taught; she spoke, typed and used shorthand in three different languages. In her younger days she managed to work as a personal assistant to a number of high-ranking politicians in Damascus, which was where I spent the first ten years of my life. I recall starting my primary education at a French school, L'école Laïque, which was walking distance from where we lived, but the school was unfortunately closed after the six-day Arab-Israeli War that took place in June 1967. I still recall the tanks stationed outside our apartment building during that time. So many things changed for my family after this conflict and eventually, for a number of reasons, we all moved to Kuwait for a new start. First my father, then mother, a year later myself and then another year later my brother joined us.

At the time, Kuwait was one of the wealthiest oil countries in the Middle East, and it was there that my education changed from French to English, in a school which is still going strong today. The New English School was founded in 1969 by a visionary couple, a Kuwaiti man and his British wife. The curriculum was taught primarily by British teachers and over a relatively short period the school began preparing its students for O-level and A-level exams. My mother was a strong believer in education and we always had the best schools chosen for us, despite the fact that our means were, at best, moderate. Consequently, a good portion of who we are, of how we live and what we believe — my brother, sister and I — is owed to her. I still remember the first time we joined that school one summer. It was on the grounds of a large villa, possibly an embassy, where they had an outdoor swimming pool that I still remember swimming in. We would get changed inside the building and walk as a class to the outdoor pool which was built up off the ground like a large concrete tank, and we would dive into it. The joy of swimming at this school is something I still recall to this day.

At some point my mother realised that people who were aiming for a high-quality education were sending their children to Lebanon, so in 1973 my brother and I were sent to a boarding school there. This must have been a very big and brave decision for our parents. Fortunately, my older brother was much more streetwise than me and he was entrusted to look after us both! First, we went to a nunnery for the summer, a boarding school run by nuns. Here we were taught mainly French, but this also gave us an introduction to beautiful Lebanon. We had many school trips and I even remember watching my first Bruce Lee film, *Fist of Fury*, that summer, and for whatever reason the image of a gold Lamborghini is firmly etched in my mind. Lebanon was after all the French Riviera of the Middle East. When term started, we joined Brummana High School. This was a beautiful (and expensive) school situated on the mountain overlooking Beirut. The school had been founded by the Quakers and also had an English-based curriculum. We were there for two years and it was at this school I sat my O-level exams. Unfortunately, in October 1973, and while we were just settling at Brummana High, another Arab-Israeli war broke out. I still recall peering up at the sky from the school grounds with fascination, watching fighter jets chase each other, though I had no clue what was going on. The war did not last long and fortunately it did not have any immediate impact on our education or our safety.

By 1975 I was getting ready for those O-levels, when everyone at school started noticing heavy guns and various bits of military equipment settling on the mountainsides near the school. Then just a few weeks before our exams, in April, the civil war in Lebanon broke out. We were mostly locked in at school, but, despite the mayhem, the uncertainty and danger, we were still able to sit our exams. However, by the end of the exam period the situation in Lebanon had become extremely dangerous and we were trapped at school even though term had finished. I don't recall all the details, but we were not able leave the grounds of the school because of all the warring factions. The Palestinian forces, the various Lebanese forces and the Syrian forces all had roadblocks. At these roadblocks one of the most sinister and depressing aspects of the war would take place: innocent people were being summarily executed based on their identity. It was rumoured that if someone were stopped at a roadblock without an ID card, the militia men would ask the person to pronounce the word "tomato"; because of the various dialects, each faction pronounced the word differently. How you pronounced the word tomato literally meant life or death. My parents were extremely worried, as we ticked the wrong boxes for most of these roadblocks. We were Muslim, carried Jordanian passports and were born in Syria! That civil war proved to be very violent, but we were extremely fortunate when for a couple of weeks, a truce allowed my brother and I to travel to Syria, all the way by taxi, to join our parents. It was just over a hundred-kilometre journey and we had to borrow the taxi fare from our maths teacher. We left in a hurry and we escaped with only our passports. We did return to Lebanon a few years later to collect our belongings from the school. I recall sitting in the back of the car looking at all the destroyed buildings riddled with bullet holes. The image of Beirut at the time can perhaps best be likened to that of bombed-out Sarajevo. That Riviera version of the place had disappeared. After escaping from Lebanon, we returned to Kuwait where two years later I completed my A-levels at my old school. I was doing relatively well in my studies and so I applied and was accepted to study medicine in the UK, at Dundee.

August 1977 was the first time I ever left home on my own. I remember landing at Heathrow and staying the night at one of the airport hotels as we had missed the connecting flight. I arrived at the hotel very late, I had no clue how to order room service and I ended up going to sleep feeling hungry and lonely. That was my first night away from home! Early next morning I took my flight to Edinburgh. It is difficult to put the experience of my first day in the UK into words. Everything I was seeing was new to me, there was a great deal to take in and I felt overwhelmed. At Edinburgh airport, I asked the taxi driver to take me to the train station as I knew I had to take a train to Dundee. I had never been to such a massive railway station before. As I arrived at Waverley train station, I recall seeing so many trains for the first time in my life. The thought of ending up lost on a train somewhere in Scotland was very daunting and I just sat in the taxi. Eventually I asked the driver if he could take me all the way to Dundee and I gave him the address, Belmont Hall of Residence. He was very happy to oblige! Two hours later we arrived at Dundee, but to my surprise, the driver did not know where Belmont Hall was and he needed to ask for directions! Finally, I was safely dropped off at my halls of residence to start what would be six years of medical studies in Dundee. As soon as I entered my room, I just fell onto my bed and started crying. It wasn't the journey that had been the most distressing, it was the fact that when I arrived in Dundee, I could not understand anyone I spoke to. Yes, it sounded as if they were speaking English, but not the English I learned at school; Scottish English was something else entirely. In case you are wondering, the taxi fare cost me twenty pounds that day!

Neither of my parents were university educated, so when I left home to study medicine, my mother had little idea what it meant in practical terms. I was her pride and joy, and she thought that once I graduated that I would therefore be qualified, and I could go back home and start working as a doctor straightaway. Just six years at the most, and I would be home. Unbeknownst to any of us at the time was that, having graduated, I needed to go through a further training programme; a degree in medicine is no more than a starting point. I graduated in 1983 and started my training in Dundee. By 1988, eleven years after leaving home, I completed my basic surgical training and I managed to obtain my surgical diploma.

Unfortunately, during my time at university, my mother was diagnosed with leukaemia. Initially this was under control and I recall her optimism as she travelled to various centres in Lebanon, the US and the UK for treatment. Sadly, as predicted, and after seven years of battling, her condition started to get out of control. I remember in March of that year, my father called me to say that mum was in hospital and that she was quite ill. This was not unusual, but this was the first time that he said we should travel over to see her. Doing so, however, was far from straightforward. It posed some administrative obstacles in view of the fact that I was still a foreign national, so I could not just get on a plane and leave and expect to easily return. I had to send my passport away for a re-entry visa, and the process took a few weeks. Eventually I arrived with my brother back in Kuwait on 08 April 1988 and our uncle picked us up from the airport. Not much was said in the car, but as we were getting close to home, my uncle told us that our mother had passed away earlier that same day. I never managed to see her alive again. It was my birthday the following day and I went to see my mother in the mortuary, for the last time, before burying her in the afternoon. I remember meeting my Uncle George at the mortuary where we bid farewell to her. He was inconsolable; I still remember his crying. At home, my father just kept quiet. In a sense, even though my mother was the architect of everything that she wished for me to be, sadly she passed away before she could see it all come good.

Shortly after that, my career almost came to a halt as I struggled to obtain a higher surgical-training post. If you cannot get such a training post, then you are no longer on the ladder to becoming a consultant. It took me another three years, but in 1991 I had my lucky break; I managed to get a temporary training post. However, those intervening three years of 1988 to 1991 had been by far the most difficult of my life, emotionally, professionally and financially. Unfortunately, the recession that kicked off in the second half of 1990 caused me to lose my house, but at least I was able to move into hospital accommodation. My self-esteem and self-belief were at an all-time low and I believe that a lot of how I approach adversity now, the resilience that I have, comes from me coping on my own through those years. I had graduated in 1983, but by 1991, after eight years of employment, all I had to show for it was a car, a stereo system, and a debt of £8000. But at least I was now back, even if only temporarily, on the training ladder.

What probably altered my fortunes for the better was getting British citizenship in 1991. Up until then, each time I applied for a job I presented myself as Jordanian, and I got nowhere. The very first time I presented myself as British I was offered an interview. Maybe that was just a coincidence, but anyhow I got a short-term job as a locum tutor in orthopaedics at the University of Manchester. For the first time since 1988 I was employed in an academic post. Getting this job gave me an immense feeling of satisfaction and a belief that I still had a chance at career success. I first started working in Manchester at Ancoats Hospital, which sadly no longer exists, and it was during that year that I bought my first computer and I started producing academic work. 1991 was a fantastic year for me. I worked my way up financially, getting back on my feet again and, on a personal level, that year gave me the belief that no matter how low things can get, given time, patience and perseverance, there is always a chance. My chance came after nearly 300 applications and I was determined to make the most out of this break.

I had my second lucky break when the one-year locum tutor post was extended to 18 months. I then got a third break when I worked for a year in research alongside an incredible Senior Lecturer who was very supportive. But then came the most incredible break in my career, which was Calmanisation. The postgraduate training structure in the

NHS was being overhauled and, in simple terms, in order to streamline the training journey of medical graduates at registrar level, two major changes took place. Firstly, training centres needed to restructure themselves to provide a comprehensive five-year training programme. Secondly, and most important to me, once you had a Calman number, you were in line to compete for a consultant post. In 1994, and with the support of my Senior Lecturer, I was offered one of these Calman numbers.

When I started working in Manchester, I was living in hospital accommodation. I first lived in a bedroom, then I had my own ensuite, and by 1993 I managed to move into a rented flat. By then I had paid off my debt and was gradually getting back on my feet financially. But still, I was single, living by myself, and I felt I needed to settle down. As with most Eastern cultures, it is the mother who usually takes on the matchmaker role. With my mother having passed away, I needed the help of my aunt in Syria. Eventually I contacted her and said something along the lines of "I want to settle down and to get married, and I need you to find someone suitable for me". This probably came as a bit of a shock to her, but she was happy with the idea and understandably she asked what I was looking for; a strange conversation to be reading about in the West in the 21st century, I know. My instinctive reply anyway was "As long as she's pretty". I guess anybody would say that. But I also said, "I need her to be a good practicing Muslim". For a few years I felt that I had been drifting away from Islam, that I had become a little wayward, and I was not comfortable with that. To my surprise, before long I received a call from my aunt telling me that she had found someone she wanted to introduce me to, so off I went on a flight to Damascus. At 33 years of age, it was a very odd experience for me to be going with my father and my uncle to meet this family in order to be introduced to their daughter. I remember meeting the young lady and her family and I liked her very much. Having gone through the proper formalities, both she and her family were happy for us to become engaged, so that we could get to know each other better before taking the big plunge. However, as soon as I returned to the UK, I received a message from my sister informing me that they had already fallen out with the family and the engagement was broken off. How strange, you might think, but this exciting journey was very short lived. A few months later my aunt called to say, "We found you another potential bride", so again I hopped on a plane to Damascus and again I met a lovely young lady, with a lovely family and we agreed to get to know each other. I came back to the UK with rekindled excitement and hope, but a few weeks later she informed me fairly bluntly "You know something, I don't think you are the right person for me, let's call it a day". This time the roles had been reversed and I was unceremoniously 'dumped'.

I started doubting if my approach to finding the love of my life would ever work. A short while later I received a phone call from my sister who said yet again "We found somebody", and I thought here we go again, but she was determined and very excited, saying "No, we *really* found someone. Get on a plane right now." This must be July or August 1993. Considering how my sister sounded on the phone, I was again very excited, but I had to keep my hopes in check. I sorted out a flight and arrived in Damascus on a Wednesday, early September, to find my sister still very excited. She told me about the girl that she met, speaking very highly of her, and that she lived in the neighbourhood just a few houses away from my aunt's house. She kept saying that there was something special about this girl, called Syrsa. So, on Thursday I went with my aunt and sister to meet the girl's family. Syrsa, wearing her headscarf, came in briefly to serve us the coffee and then stepped out. She looked absolutely gorgeous and I politely smiled and said that the coffee was very good, only for her to say it was her mother that made it! When we reminisce about our first encounter, Syrsa tells me that she was in fact not very excited about our visit. It is traditional that when meeting a suiter, on the first visit the girl will come in for a few minutes, and then step out. The rest of the family, especially her parents, will get to know as much about you and your family as they can, and then you hope that they will get back to you should their daughter decide that she would be happy to speak to you! Friday we were all waiting for her mother to call and hopefully say that we could come back for a second visit. We waited and waited, and finally we received a call late in the afternoon where her mother informed my aunt that Syrsa was happy to meet with me for another chat. I was over the moon.

The following day I went alone and knocked at the door. I don't remember who opened the door for me, but I ended up sitting with Syrsa in that same room on our own for about three hours. It did not feel awkward to either of us, and we just kept on talking about ourselves; well, mostly about myself. I think I fell for her straight away and I could see why my sister was so excited about this girl. When I met her that day, my heart was pounding so hard but somehow, I managed to keep it together. I went again the following day and we chatted for over four hours before we parted company. I suppose she had heard enough by then and both of us had a decision to make, but I had a deep feeling in my heart that this was going to be the one. I could not describe it, but something about her felt exceptional and I was hoping and praying that she thought I was the one for her as well.

On the Monday, just a few days after we first met, I asked my father and my aunt to formally request Syrsa's hand in marriage and on Tuesday the answer came back as yes, Syrsa has agreed. Wow! I was absolutely beyond myself.

The following few days were extremely hectic as we needed to sort out the necessary paperwork for the registry office. We were officially married a week later. I remember it was a difficult day because we had to find an office that could register the marriage, but that day was a public holiday and everywhere was closed. We eventually found an office that agreed to register the marriage in a nearby little town. My father, Syrsa, her brother and I all went to register the marriage on 14 September 1993, after which we had a modest family gathering. I was in a desperate hurry because as soon as we got married, I needed to start a visa application for her. By then, I was a British national, but Syrsa was Syrian. It was tricky convincing the British Consulate official that we were truly married having met just over a week ago. Just like me, they were having some difficulty believing that this had really happened. It was amazing, it was like a wonderful dream, I was married, and it was all a whirlwind. When Syrsa asks me about those days I tell her that I honestly cannot remember much of the detail and everything still feels like a dream. In fact, she is the one that reminded me of what took place.

When I look back at that fateful week, I cannot help but be grateful that Syrsa saw something in me that convinced her to take such a decision. Financially, I was not fully on my feet yet, but she later said to me that what struck her about me was honesty and humility. She had many suiters before me, but she felt comfortable and safe with me. Now and again, she teases me about who her suitors were before I came along, saying she married me because I needed looking after!

We did eventually manage to sort out the visa application and everything felt as if it was falling nicely into place. Having only taken two weeks off work, I had to get back, and sadly there was not enough time to arrange a proper wedding. In next to no time, I was on a plane back to Manchester, by myself but married. Syrsa arrived a couple of months later. She had her previous commitments too, of course, such as completion of her MSc in Microbiology and she needed to sort out many things because she had never expected in her wildest dreams that she would be leaving Damascus for good. She did actually manage to have what one would call a 'girl's wedding' with all her friends and family, but I was not there. In fact, we never actually had a wedding, and our 'wedding' photos were taken when we returned to Damascus together. I had promised Syrsa's mother that we would travel back within three months, and we had a mini celebration then. When Syrsa joined me in Manchester, she completed another MSc in Microbiology at the University of Manchester before starting to apply for a training post, but she couldn't get anywhere. After a number of applications, she decided that she was probably better off putting her energy elsewhere. In fact, her struggle finding a training post brought back painful memories of my own journey. When I speak to her about that decision, she tells me that she was happy with it and that she never felt that her role was compromised.

I passed my speciality exam in 1997 and received my certificate of completion of training, and I became a consultant in 1998. Four years later we moved to Hale Barns, where we have been living since. Within a few months of moving here I got to know many of the people at our local Islamic Centre. As I became more involved with the community, I eventually joined the committee of the

Altrincham Muslim Association, where I later served as chairman. I started taking the time to learn more about Islam, so my knowledge of Islam progressed, particularly when I began teaching as part of a study circle. When we were married, Syrsa's knowledge of Islam was far better than mine, but with her support I gradually picked up. I started delivering sermons at our centre and over time I gained a good standing within my community. I later became involved in interfaith work, getting to know our local synagogues and churches. I regularly represented my mosque on Remembrance Sunday, for example, first attending the Sunday service at All Saints Church before I would proceed with the vicar to the Hale Barns war memorial. There we gathered with other local vicars and rabbis for an interfaith memorial service. We then all proceeded to a buffet at the neighbouring synagogue. I also had the privilege of serving as the mayor's chaplain for two years, where one of my duties was to open the council meetings with a prayer. These meetings took place on a Wednesday evening after my clinic. I would dash over there in the car arriving just in time to give the prayer, and I would occasionally stay and observe these meetings as I found the political ramblings invariably amusing. I built a number of lasting friendships over these two years.

I suppose all this is to say that by the time of 2017 when I was attacked, perhaps I was not just some random guy. I was well known in the area, in my community, my local churches and synagogues, from my work at the hospital and with our local council. Still, I had never felt like I was, or could be, a target. Until, of course, that fateful day.

Chapter 2

The Attack

It was Sunday, 24 September 2017. We had a committee meeting at the Islamic Centre I attend which was scheduled to take place immediately after Asr prayers, the mid-afternoon prayers, at 17:30. As it was towards the end of September, there was a fair bit of gardening to be done, and that meant being home for longer on a Sunday doing what was necessary with the garden. Consequently, I was running slightly late, so when I got into my car and saw the time was just short of 17:30, I knew I would be a couple of minutes late. I drove along Hale Road, down Delahays Road and onto Grove Lane, a short journey of only a few minutes from home. Along Grove Lane, as I approached the Centre, I looked for a place to park but by then most places were already taken. I drove further up the road, turned back, and eventually found a place on the opposite side not too far from the Centre, probably about a hundred yards or so. I locked the car, went to cross the road—I parked on a narrow strip with a bend so had to look carefully as I crossed—and walked past a few houses before entering the mosque. We don't normally refer to the Centre as a mosque as essentially it is a community cultural centre, with just part of it used for prayers. Originally, it was a church known as St. David's. Built in 1915, it is already past its centenary and probably it is well beyond its sell-by date, so to speak. The centre has two buildings: the daily prayer hall on the left-hand side as you go up the entrance path, then towards the end of the path is the larger back building; our activity hall. For the five daily prayers we routinely used the smaller left-hand hall. At the front of the Centre there is a set of waist-high iron gates, a number of iron fence panels and a few mature trees. The two buildings are set on a slight elevation, so you have to walk up a slope between the entrance gates and the hall doors. We had CCTV cameras installed a few years ago following several racially motivated attacks.

Having crossed the road, and as I was walking towards the Centre, I spotted someone on the other side of the road no more than 50 yards away. At the time, this seemed innocuous, and probably the only reason I noticed him was because he was the only person around on that quiet road. Perhaps if there had been more people then I might have been distracted by them, but I clearly recall he was the only person I saw. I do not remember if he looked back at me, but everything seemed entirely normal. From that glance I recall noticing that he was tall enough to have his head above the car he was next to. As I turned away from him, I remember sensing that he was about to cross the road. It seemed that as soon as he saw me walking towards the centre, he crossed the road and walked towards me. I do not remember at what stage he passed me, and I only vaguely sensed that someone was there. It was just something normal that you do every day walking down the road. You sense people walking towards you and past you but there is no eye contact, and you don't stare. In any case, I was focused on rushing to the mosque, knowing I was already late.

But then I recall a silly thing that I did as I passed the last house before the Centre's gates. Because of my newly acquired interest in gardening, I had started looking at other people's gardens to get some ideas; I would look to see what they had planted and how the garden is landscaped. As I passed the front garden of this house, for whatever reason I remember being critical of some brickwork that had been done. Basically, it was just a very ordinary Sunday. Eventually, I entered the front gate which is invariably kept open during prayer times, and I started walking up the path, a clear path with little of note. But then out of the blue, and this is one thing I have never really been able to articulate, it still seems somewhat indescribable, but I felt a sudden, massive pain. I described it once as seeming like somebody had put a hammer drill into the back of my neck. I do not know why, but it was as if the pain had a sound and that is perhaps the best way I can describe it. At the time, in that instant, and I do not really know why, I imagined I was hit by a baseball bat. It seems to have been an instantaneous rationalisation, probably a reflection of watching too many films and crime series. Whatever it was, there was no doubt that it felt extremely painful. I also recall that as the pain struck, I was thrust forwards, but still with no clue what the hell just happened to me. It was not so much frightening at that point; it was simply extremely painful and nothing else. I did not even notice the presence of someone who had snuck up behind me, and I think on reflection I was somewhat fortunate. Fortunate because if you experience a horrendous event, some of the lasting emotional and psychological trauma can come from events leading up to the physical pain, from the anticipation of harm, from seeing the weapon and from the experience of helplessness and fear, for example. Perhaps if I had experienced such emotions leading up to the stabbing, they may have had a lasting impact on me. In that sense, I was lucky, it was sudden, but nevertheless I was thrust quickly into a different world.

With nobody immediately in view, in all my naivety my next thought was that a tree branch had fallen on me. I looked around to see where the tree was, where the branch was, because this surely was the only thing that could have hit me, but there was nothing there. Then as I turned, there was this man, and I saw his face. It had been a couple of seconds, but I still could not figure out what had happened; even when I saw him, I still had no idea. Despite the horrendous pain in my neck and this man appearing just behind me, it did not occur to me that he had struck me. It took me probably another couple of seconds, the two of us just standing there, me still looking for a tree branch, but, of course, there was nothing, just him. I wasn't yet sure, but I was starting to realise it must have been him just because there was nothing else around. All I was looking at was his face, and I remember from the corner of my eye I glimpsed something metallic under his right arm. I later realised that this was just the frame of the iron gate and not what I instinctively thought, which was that he might have hit me with an iron bar. Throughout these few seconds, I never noticed his hand and never saw the knife held there. Again, perhaps that was a blessing because if I had seen a knife my reaction might well have been different.

We stood there with no more than a couple of yards between us and I remember his face, at least I remember what I started to see in his face. He was angry. There was no doubt about that, he was very angry, almost animal-like as if he was baring his teeth. He shouted at me, he used the f-word I remember, but then he said something else. I wasn't fully registering what he was saying, I was looking at his body language rather than listening to him, instinctively asking myself what he might want to do. But then I believe he said, "This is for what you've done!" I have tried to make sense of that statement since, but I cannot even be sure if that was exactly what he shouted at me, never mind why. Perhaps I will know one day. Nonetheless, it is this phrase that has stuck with me, though in all honesty I could not put my hand on the Bible and swear by Almighty God that this was exactly what was said.

I still wasn't aware that he had just stabbed me though, only that I had pain in my neck, but then his anger gripped me, and it seemed that he was poised to do something else again. He moved towards me and at that moment it became clear to me that he meant further harm. That said, the phrase "became clear" does not really tell the whole story. It was an instinctive inner sense rather than a logical thought process. In such a situation there is no time for thinking. My instinct told me that something is not right, that this person did something bad, and even though I still did not realise there was a knife, instinctively I turned around and ran away as fast as I could. I think the speed I ran at is something I only realised subsequently because my legs were still hurting three days later from that sprint. I think I must have run at what was for me some exceptional speed, and I just ran in a straight line, directly away from him.

The people who were in the Centre praying, who could have helped me, were on my left-hand side, but I didn't even think of turning to the left because that would have taken time. My instinct was to run in a straight line, so I ran the 20 yards or so to the back main hall. Not that I was expecting anybody to be there, I was not so much running for help, I just ran. There were a few steps to climb and I think I cleared them with a single jump, whereupon I reached the entrance. The time between me turning from the attack and arriving at that door was probably no more than three to four seconds. The back hall has a large pair of solid wooden doors that are normally kept shut. On that afternoon, fortunately, these doors were open, but then immediately on entering you face another entrance door, a glass door with an upper frosted panel and a self-closing hinge. There is no lock on this door, but it only opens outwards! As I reached this door, I had to stop. I vividly remember that moment of realising that I would have to stop running. I had to pause and take a step back to be able to open the door. The moment that I had to stop running away was the most distinctive for me in the whole scenario. It was probably no more than a split second, but as I realised that I would have to open the door outwards, that was the moment where I actually felt the fear. As I stopped to open the door, even without knowing whether he was following behind me or not, I feared for my life; I was petrified. I still recall the thoughts that raced through my mind: I needed to hide, where could I hide? I don't remember ever feeling so petrified in my life. I pulled the door back and as I entered I immediately saw two women in the hall.

That was when something amazing happened to me. As suddenly as it had gripped me, in that split second, the fear suddenly disappeared. I have no idea how my instincts took over, but on reflection it is most likely that my instincts dictated that I had to protect these two women. It was not that I felt safe or reassured by their presence, but I believe that I went from being afraid to being protective. To me, the presence of these two women in the hall when I entered was a life-changing moment. It may seem strange to claim that, but I truly believe that I may have ended up as a totally different person if they had not been there. I knew what being petrified felt like and I think it would have taken me a long time to be able to confront and to overcome such fear, if I could have done so at all. I still cannot explain it, but as soon as I saw these two women, the fear simply vanished. All this took place within the space of a few seconds and as far as my experience with running away and with fear went, it was done.

As soon as I saw them, I think I shouted, "Call the police!" and I grabbed a chair and ran back towards the door. I was determined that he was not going to come in. That was the overwhelming issue with the presence of these two women. Perhaps the fact that I felt this way, with that determination, is what completely changed my attitude and took away the fear. I ran out and I saw that he was no longer there. He was gone; a few seconds of my life and that was it, he was not there anymore. I looked around a bit more to make sure he was not hiding, but there really seemed to be no-one around. Later, at the trial, I saw the CCTV footage, and I saw that he had ran after me. But then a few seconds later I think he might have realised that there could have been more people inside. CCTV showed him running out of the Centre's grounds, back in the direction he had come from.

Once I became confident there was no-one around, I went inside again, I put the chair down, paused, and then that horrendous pain started to really take effect. The two women asked me what happened, but all I could tell them was that someone had hit me. I think they themselves had a look outside and didn't see anyone and then probably rushed to the prayer hall and called the others for help. Quite quickly, people started to come into the back hall where I was. By then, I was sitting on one of the wooden benches at the back of the hall grabbing tightly onto my neck. The pain was horrendous; I felt that if I were to let go of my neck that my head was going to fall off. I remember someone grabbing my right wrist to check my pulse and someone else asking me what had happened and if I could describe who attacked me. Still, there wasn't any obvious wound or mark visible. But then someone wanted to have a look at my neck so they asked if I could let my left hand go. It was a struggle to let go. I slowly raised my head and made sure my neck was straight and gradually I was able to take my hand off. It was then that I heard: "You've been stabbed in the neck."

I don't recall clearly what immediately went through my mind when I heard that. I did not experience anxiety or panic. I simply looked at my left hand and saw there was no blood. I was able to move everything in both arms, my fingers, my wrists and my elbows. There was no tingling or heaviness anywhere in my body. My breathing was normal and so was my voice. I remember saying "I am OK", "Alhamdullilah (praise the Lord) I am OK." My surgical and trauma training seemed to have spontaneously kicked in, and even though I did not know where exactly the entry wound was, I knew straight away that none of the vital structures in my neck were damaged. I was able to reassure myself and others that there was no need to panic.

I was not aware that during this period someone started filming me on their phone and producing what would later become the short video that was circulated online. The video was no more than a couple of minutes long, but it did capture the moment. I still watch it with a sense of joy and relief as I believe it was a good reflection of me and I am just really glad I did not say or do something too embarrassing. I know I am a fairly level-headed and serious person, but I also like a laugh and I cannot help myself using a cliché now and again. When I realised I had been stabbed, I was heard saying on the video "The bastard got me in the neck." This was later relayed back to me from a friend who said her little child told her "Uncle Nasser said a bad word." That was probably one of the most embarrassing moments of the entire event; an Imam using the "B*" word. I remember that I asked ITV who requested permission to air the video to be kind enough to bleep or remove the "B*" word. It was a great relief when I watched the video on TV the following day and true to their promise, the "B*" word was gone.

So, there I was sat on the bench, again grabbing my neck firmly having realised that I had been stabbed. Unbeknownst to anyone, I had just been off work for a week on study leave to attend the annual British Orthopaedic Association conference. This week off meant that I had literally hundreds of emails to get back to. If I end up taking another week off, I thought to myself, I might end up with even twice as many emails on my return. I resolved there and then to not take any time off, silly as it may sound, but by then this is what was running through my mind, the fact that I need to go back to work the following day. I'm not sure if thinking about the next day is a consequence of the shock of what had just happened to me, but I do recall that at some point I started thinking ahead about my immediate future, probably convincing myself that there was indeed going to be an immediate future. I don't know. Perhaps I was just not looking forward to hundreds of emails.

There was no external evidence of significant bleeding, but even so a few minutes down the line I started feeling a little faint and I knew I needed to lie down on the floor. I was aware that feeling faint was not unusual now that the adrenaline rush was winding down. The most important thing for me was to lie down and get blood to my head before I ended up fainting altogether. So, I was not so much worried about fainting, but I was also feeling a little bit queasy. I did have a minor concern in that I had just eaten before leaving home, and I knew very well that if I didn't get down on the floor quickly, I might throw up. I really did not want to do that. I untied my belt to get comfortable, I started to breath slowly, I lay down on the floor and turned onto my right side, in a sense doing my own airway protection drill in case I did faint and throw up. In just short of a minute, it was a great relief that the sickly feeling passed and I no longer felt faint. A few moments later, the police and ambulance crew arrived.

Still the magnitude of the event had not really dawned on me. I was in my little bubble and apart from that horrendous constant pain, I was somewhat fine. The paramedic arrived and the time came for them to put a drip in my arm. Of course, it is standard procedure to put that big needle in the arm, but of all things, I hate needles. Anyway, I said to the paramedic "It's OK", I opened my right arm and held my breath, and fortunately the paramedic was brilliant, I felt nothing. They wanted to immobilise me like they would do for a suspected blunt neck injury, but I reassured them that I did not have a blunt neck injury and there is no likelihood of me having suffered a broken neck. Anyhow, standard procedure carried on and I was put in a scoop. As they were about to carry me away, I remember people saying they needed to inform my wife, and I said, "Please don't, please don't tell her anything yet." I just could not bear the thought that she wasn't in a position to know what had happened to me, and to know that I'm physically and emotionally okay. I did not want her to be upset, but I later found out that by the time I was scooped, she had already been made aware of the attack. So, there I was on a funny little trip to the ambulance parked just outside the Centre, strapped into this narrow flimsy scoop, having to cede all control. As we went down those four steps that I earlier cleared with one jump the scoop felt wobbly, and I wondered if I was going to fall out. Soon I was being secured in the back of the ambulance. That drive was not a comfortable ride by any measure. It was an experience; the siren, the flashing lights and flying through the streets with no concept of time or direction, but I was not physically comfortable. Very soon, the back doors of the ambulance were flung open, and I was carried into Wythenshawe Hospital, my hospital.

Chapter 3

Hospital

This is insider information, but if you are unfortunate enough to be stabbed in Manchester, it is very likely that you would be rushed to Manchester Royal infirmary. This is neither my local hospital nor the hospital I work at and I did not want to end up there. I had somewhat cheekily asked the ambulance crew if they would take me to my local hospital. It was my decision, and I wanted to be treated where everyone knew me. By the time the ambulance arrived at the hospital I was no longer strapped to the scoop looking at the ceiling. I was now sitting slightly up, starting to get a sense of my surroundings.

As per protocol, the ambulance crew would have called in the incident and the trauma team were waiting, ready to receive the injured victim. The team would normally include one of my orthopaedic trainees, but it also happened that at the time, one of my consultant colleagues was attending the emergency department along with the on-duty orthopaedic registrar. I did not expect that they would be present, but equally, no one had a clue who the victim was. Later, my consultant colleague informed me that on that afternoon, she was about to leave but decided instead to wait in order to make sure her services were not required. She was not prepared for the shock that would hit her. No one was. As I was wheeled into the resuscitation room the stretcher gradually turned around and I came face to face with my colleague and trainees standing side by side. I instinctively smiled at them, but all I could see was three white faces, wide eyed and totally stunned. The site of my junior trainee was unforgettable. His jaw literally dropped, and I watched his face turn white. They were totally dumbfounded, but they rushed to hold my hand and comfort me. The reality was that they also needed some comforting, some reassurance that I was alright. The shock on their faces at that moment was priceless, but in that moment I could see what they meant to me and what I meant to them, and I was grateful to be there with them.

It did not take long before we all had to snap out of this emotional encounter and start acting professionally. After all, there was a potentially critically injured patient in need of emergency assessment and care. Despite their initial resistance, colleagues were formally asked to vacate the resuscitation area while the accident and emergency team took over in order to begin their standard 'resus' protocol. They were very professional and equally courteous. For a victim with a penetrating injury, the immediate imperative is to make sure that there is no imminent threat to life. This may sound gruesome, but it is essentially making sure that a) the victim is breathing soundly and b) not bleeding to death. Once these are checked, the examination then follows a well-defined structured and systematic sequence to determine the nature and extent of the 'primary' damage. In essence, this involves looking for the immediate damage caused by the knife penetrating my neck. The young A&E doctor proceeded to examine me, much as I did in my own assessment earlier. Of course, he had to get it right and to his credit he did not seem to be phased by the fact that he was examining a senior colleague, knowing full well that his own competence was also being assessed! By the end of his examination, it was reassuring to learn that I had not missed anything earlier! The nurse took my vital signs again — pulse, blood pressure and oxygen saturation — before starting to prepare another intravenous drip. It was simply not my day. The A&E doctor had the last laugh. Once he finished his assessment he smiled at me and said, "I need to put another needle in your left arm." I remembered why; for a penetrating injury, two large bore cannulas, one in each arm, is the standard Advanced Trauma Life Support (ATLS) protocol. After all, I was an ATLS instructor, and I should have seen it coming. For the second time that day I opened my arm and held my breath.

It was a very unusual experience for me to be on the receiving end of an examination that I had so often carried out and to see how this young A&E doctor was trying to reassure me and keep me calm about what he was doing and why. Once he cleared my arms and legs, he asked me to lean forward so he could examine the back of my neck. He told me the wound did not look dirty and was not bleeding much, nonetheless I still needed to have a tetanus jab, so that meant, yes, another needle. With my surgical background, I knew very early that the penetrating knife has missed all the vital structures in my neck, but I also knew that I had to go through a rigorous examination just the same. I wasn't frightened or distressed, and I found myself reassuring others that apart from the pain, I was feeling fine and calm. Perhaps if I was not a doctor, I would have felt very different. But there I was, in very familiar surroundings and with people that I knew, going through their usual business, all of which was very comforting for me. Even though I was aware that so far I was 'clinically stable', I knew that the A&E doctor would still consider me to be in a potentially critical condition. The potential for secondary life-threatening internal damage needed to be excluded before I would be off the critical list.

Once he finished his initial assessment, the young doctor informed me that I would soon be going for a CT scan of my neck, and he left the bay. As he left, a young, awkward-looking police officer entered and requested a statement. I had been expecting to see the police at some stage, but I wasn't sure why this particular officer looked out of sorts, uncomfortable and anxious. It was the first inkling I had that there were perhaps wider implications of the attack. I cannot recall exactly how the conversation went, but I remember he wanted me to go through the incident in as much detail as I could recall. Unfortunately, his awkwardness only increased during this questioning when Syrsa walked in. The questions just stopped, or probably I just stopped listening to them. I looked at Syrsa's face and I could see she was calm. She wasn't pale, she wasn't hyperventilating, she wasn't anxious, she just walked towards me and held my hand. I told her I was okay and she nodded to say "I know you are". Her immediate words were "I'm so grateful to God". I think when she first saw me, she could immediately tell there was nothing horribly wrong as I was sat up talking to the officer. It was probably that first eye contact as she entered. Perhaps I smiled and shook my head. She is a doctor herself, and when she saw me sat up on the trolley, she saw for herself that I was OK. We did not say much to each other; I was alright, and probably that was all that mattered.

The officer just stood there waiting for his moment to barge in, which he eventually did. But then it came to that critical question, "Do you remember what he said to you?" Up to that point, I never really thought about what my attacker said to me. It was then that I had to start remembering what was shouted at me as it might give a clue to why I was attacked. I clearly remembered walking onto the grounds of the mosque, I clearly recalled the moment of sudden pain and I clearly recalled the look on his face, but for the life of me, at that moment, I could not recall exactly what he said. As I struggled to remember, I think I mentioned to the officer that I recall he swore at me. Then I think I said that he had uttered one sentence, just one sentence, and that was all that I could come up with. Somehow, I found it difficult to recall his exact words and I wasn't sure why. I told the officer that I needed some time to remember. To be honest, I was somewhat disappointed with myself that I could not recall what had been said. But even then, I was conscious of the fact that I should not put words into someone else's mouth, and I needed to be careful as to what I might say. I may have told the officer that I would need to think this through more carefully and it would probably be the following day before I could complete my statement. But then came yet another embarrassing moment for a victim. The police officer asked me to get undressed and to give him my clothing as it was now 'material evidence'. I proceeded to get undressed and gave him my shirt, my trousers, my belt and my socks. Fortunately, my underpants did not qualify as material evidence. Syrsa was not happy at all; the shirt and the belt were new, and they suited me! In any case, I thought what the heck, I am going to stay the night at the hospital as they would most likely need to observe me overnight. As for my shoes, I was somewhat lucky as they were still on the shelf at the mosque and thankfully they were not seized. I was now down to my underpants! I looked at Syrsa and we both laughed at the silliness of the situation as I tried to cover myself as much as I could with the flimsy trolly sheet. Syrsa then told me that around thirty people were waiting outside to make sure I was OK, and we agreed that she should go out and let everyone know that I was fine and to get the word around that the immediate worry is over. As she left, I closed my eyes and started to replay the earlier events to help me remember what the hell this young man had said to me.

Soon enough, the nurse returned to recheck my vital signs. At some stage I was given a strong analgesic for my pain, I think morphine, and it was 'titrated' in. As I saw the injection going into the cannula, I waited for that extraordinary experience of having morphine in my veins for the first time in my life. I waited in anticipation for this so called 'trip'. This would probably be the only time I could legally experience such a trip, but sadly nothing happened, one of the more disappointing aspects to that situation. Anyhow, the nurse ran some more fluid through the cannula and everyone was ready for me to go to the CT scanner. This was the only trip I had that evening!

A CT scan is standard protocol for a penetrating injury. The scan is necessary to identify the depth of the injury and to check for internal bleeding, which is bleeding that does not gush out through the wound but stays inside the body and can put pressure on, and so cause damage to, vital structures. A few minutes later I was wheeled into the scanner room and was asked to slide myself from the trolly onto the narrow scanner bed. With a cannula in each arm, a drip line on the left and a painful neck, I was trying desperately to keep my dignity with this flimsy trolley sheet. But then I thought, at least for this night, I should just be a patient and give up on being 'dignified'; it can't get any worse. As part of the scan routine, a contrast dye needs to be administered through one of the cannulas. This contrast flows through the blood stream and has the ability to highlight blood vessels and so, most crucially, it can highlight internal bleeding. The protocol is for a scan sequence to be done before and after the contrast dye is injected. If there is an area of bleeding, the contrast will seep out where the bleeding is, and this can be picked up as a difference between the two scan sequences. I remember a warm feeling up my arm when the contrast went through me and I think I also felt a strange taste in my mouth, but nothing unduly unpleasant. A quick glance at my scans showed that the bleeding was very minimal and fortunately there was no major, or even minor, vessel damage. This was a big relief to everyone as the carotid and jugular vessels were very near to where I was stabbed. The smaller vertebral arteries were also missed and even the little veins that lit up on the scan were cleared by no more than a millimetre. None, absolutely none, of the important structures in my neck were harmed. The knife tore through my neck muscles with almost surgical precision, avoiding everything. The scan was quickly and formally reported as showing no primary structural damage, which I already knew, and no potential secondary damage, which was obviously good news. I was now officially off the critical list and everyone could take a deep sigh of relief. I believe my consultant colleague was soon notified, and she in turn passed the message to all my immediate work colleagues. The journey back to the resus room involved another gliding manoeuvre from the scanner bed onto the trolly, but by now I didn't care much about the effectiveness of the trolly sheet.

Soon I was back in the resus room, where the A&E doctor reassured me again about the scan findings. He then proceeded to clean and stitch my wound. We always say "This won't hurt much" as the local anaesthetic is being injected, and yes, I never really believed that myself entirely when I would say the same. But now I was on the receiving end, and it did hurt, even though the doctor kept on saying, with confidence, this won't hurt much. I thought "Better keep my mouth shut and not have him become more anxious than he probably already was." I still recall feeling every stitch. I thought I counted five, but later found them to be only four! I remember keeping very still and very quiet. He then asked me if I felt anything. Well, what could I say? By then Syrsa came back in to hold my hand and everyone was expecting that I would spend the night at the hospital. I was still lying there in my underpants when the A&E doctor said, "Dr Kurdy, you're all clear, you can go home now." Syrsa and I looked at each other and our immediate thought was that there was no way I was going to walk out like this! Fortunately, I was able to get a colleague to fetch me some scrubs and a pair of clogs. The cannulas were pulled out and Syrsa helped me get dressed. I sat at the edge of the trolley for a couple of minutes to make sure I didn't feel faint and then stood up and leaned on her. I felt OK; we were ready to go home.

As we were walking out along the hospital corridor and we saw friends waiting, I started to realise the commotion that was simmering out there. There were about thirty people waiting for me and I started to get a sense of how they were interpreting the attack. Now that the concerns about my health had settled, I sensed anger, and for the first time I started to feel uncomfortable. Very early on, friends were already questioning things such as why me, why at the mosque? Throughout my time at the hospital, which probably took no more than two hours, I was virtually secluded and was totally unaware of what was unfolding elsewhere. A hospital's resus room is a very particular type of place, and your mind does not take you much beyond where you are. At no time did I consider what might be happening at the mosque, never mind anywhere else. I was unaware of what the police had been doing and naïvely I had not expected the media to have been informed. However, it gradually transpired that it was nothing short of mayhem and I knew absolutely nothing about it.

I think if it hadn't been for us sending reassuring messages telling people not to come to the hospital, there would have been about three hundred people there. My stabbing had all the hallmarks of an Islamophobic hate attack. My community already felt vulnerable and under threat. The police had a potential terrorist case on their hands and the media had a story to tell. It was not taking much for people to start making up their own stories. I later found out that our Islamic centre and the police had already released official statements regarding the incident and I also became aware that an urgent meeting was planned for that evening, which would include representatives from the CPS, the police and members of the local Muslim community. Serious questions needed to be addressed: was this a planned attack on the mosque; is there an extremist background to this crime; was the immediate safety of our neighbours and the wider community at risk? I presume the police would have also been concerned about the potential backlash from such an incident. It was reassuring when I found out about this meeting and the fact that such questions were being taken seriously at a high level. It was partly as a consequence of this meeting that it was decided the attack would be officially classified as a hate crime.

By the time we arrived home, the short video taken soon after the stabbing had already been viewed in Pakistan, Jordan, Iraq, Israel, Russia, Australia and the UAE! It was on a global trip. The heading did not need much elaboration: *"Muslim Imam and surgeon stabbed in an unprovoked attack as he entered his local mosque"*. The sentiments were already heading in one direction and feelings were running high. However, as we arrived home and opened the front door, all seemed finally calm. We asked friends to give us some privacy that evening, reassuring everyone that we were fine, but we just needed time to recover and, God willing, we would take things from there the following day.

Both of my sons were at home when we got back, Ahmad is the younger, then 13, and Oaiss was 20. They both knew early on that I was OK. When we arrived home, they were calm and relaxed and already back on their computers. The house felt calm with no excitement and very little commotion. I did not feel like watching TV and Syrsa and I just wanted to sit together and get our breath back. My daughter Assma lived in London then, though at the time of the incident she was on a short break in Barcelona. She had already gotten the news and seen the short video! She needed to hear my voice and we quickly phoned to reassure her.

Even though I still felt calm, I was in agony. My neck was hurting a great deal and I had to move very slowly, taking my time, taking things easy. I sat with Syrsa in a small room next to the kitchen. Strangely, we did not feel comfortable sitting in the living room somehow, we needed to feel cosy and close to each other. Messages started to flood in via various routes. It was a surreal experience reading "Your story is now in Pakistan, you're on Pakistani TV: 'Muslim Imam Stabbed in the Mosque'", though at this point I still had no clue that there was a video. The person who recorded it was very discrete, and I don't think anyone knew about it until they were watching it later. Some of my friends were unhappy that this took place and expressed concerns that it intruded on my privacy. In all honesty, and seeing how the story eventually unfolded, I could not begrudge what he did. That short video depicted a genuine moment and genuine expression, and it became the focal point of my experience. Without it I would only have memories, and I cannot be thankful enough that these images exist. I remember speaking to my sister that evening, who lives in the UAE, but all I can recall from the conversation was her crying her heart out. She is my only sister, and she needed a great deal of comforting and calming down, especially after she saw me grabbing onto my neck in agony; the video was already there.

As we sat alone in that little room, I quickly became disinterested in what was taking place outside. Both Syrsa and I felt we were not yet ready for it all. It was distracting from what we felt was most important to us; the fact that I walked away virtually unscathed from a stabbing in the neck. I recall we sat together on our own, facing each other, and we were fairly quiet, just looking at each other and smiling. I then asked, "How do you feel?" She said, "I feel the mercy of God has touched you today." She said it in Arabic, and the word we use for mercy is رحمة. At no point did she mention anger or frustration as to why this happened to us. She never questioned "What the hell happened to you" or "Why did he pick on you"; none of that. She did not feel threatened or vulnerable. She just kept on saying "I feel the mercy of God has touched you today". But then she said something that is perhaps meaningful to people of faith but may not be fathomable by others. She said, "I feel an Angel held his hand", "his" being the attacker. That was the feeling running deep in her heart. She knew the knife could have gone anywhere in my neck, and she felt that in her heart as this man thrust the knife in me, an angel grabbed his hand. I am not sure, but I think it is fair to say that Muslims and other people of faith tend to rationalise events in their lives based on their faith and the strength of their beliefs. We believe that there is a God, we believe in angels and we believe that there is a higher purpose in life. I know that this does not sit comfortably with some people, and I also know that some may view this as downright stupid. But that is who we are. Such belief is imprinted within our psyche and makes Syrsa and I who we are. The two of us differ in many ways from each other, but when it came to faith, I told Syrsa that this was exactly how I felt. Not the slightest hint of anger came to my mind, or indeed any negativity. I just felt I was blessed, and that God was merciful to me.

But then, and as we sat there talking, Oaiss walked in. He had been at his computer and he asked us if we realised what was happening on social media. Of course, we didn't. "They're starting to get angry" he told us. I had not read much of what was being circulated online, and in all honesty, I really did not feel it was time to engage yet. However, my son's intrusion triggered something within me right there. I had sensed the anger earlier as I was leaving the hospital and now this. The calmness that we were feeling was not being mirrored by everyone else. On the contrary, it was exactly the opposite, and this did not sit well with me at all. I told my son we needed to send a message right now. It needed to be simple, clear and explicit; we did not want anyone to retaliate or to promote anger or hate. I remember that the message ended with "My father is not angry; he doesn't want anyone to be angry on his behalf." I just asked Oaiss to pass it to his friends and let them pass it on. By now, that air of contemplation and calmness was gone, and I felt very early on that I was already being forced to take a stand. If there was anger and frustration surfacing that evening, it was because of that. It just did not seem to me to be the right time to have to deal with that sort of behaviour, but there was little I could do about it. On reflection, and despite how I felt, I am grateful that this surfaced early as it had the effect of resetting my mood. Whether I liked it or not, my stabbing was somehow bigger than just 'me' and I felt I needed to step up. This changing perspective may well have had a big impact on how I started to think and behave.

Later that night we were visited by two police officers checking to see if we needed any help, probably just before midnight. We assured them that we were fine. We didn't feel scared or vulnerable and by then we were again feeling calm. It may have seemed strange, but there we were like any other day ready to go to sleep. We switched everything off and went upstairs to bed. After all, it was Monday the following day and we needed to get ready! As Syrsa went upstairs that night, she literally hit the bed and fell asleep. So did my sons. But I could not sleep. Whichever position I took in bed, within a couple of seconds I was in agony. Even though I knew how to handle my pain, still I was in agony. I tried resting on my back, my side, curling the pillow and so many other positions, but the pain just kept on banging through. To some extent I now empathise more with my patients. Previously, I would perhaps wonder what they meant by "agony", but now I knew. I think I took another couple of codeine tablets in the middle of the night and this at least eased the pain enough to allow me to think. I was trying hard to remember what this man said to me. But also, I was thinking through what could have happened if that knife had touched my spinal cord. The overwhelming sense that I had was of being grateful to Almighty God. The Arabic phrase is الحمد لله ("al-hamdulillah"), an expression meaning "All praise be to Almighty God". These two words roll easily off the tongue. Throughout the night I was repeating الحمد لله. It somewhat temporarily distracted me from the pain, until I moved again. All night I was thinking "Thank God I'm still alive, thank God it wasn't worse". But one other thought that occurred was that since the moment I was stabbed, I had not done anything good, anything thankful. To simply say "Thank God" does not really cut it, so I promised God that as soon as I woke up in the morning, I would make a donation. But before that, I still needed to fall asleep. I remember I asked God, "Help me sleep", "Come on God help me sleep". But pain is pain, and no matter what I did, I could not get into any comfortable position. My head felt so heavy and the pain went on throughout the night, until finally, about 7:00am, I dozed off.

Chapter 4

"Do You Forgive Him?"

I am still unable to fathom what made me behave in the manner I did the following day. I have tried to trace my thoughts and feelings, but I have not been able to put my finger on any specific turning point. A number of things happened early that Monday morning which may well have made my offering forgiveness inevitable. This is how the morning unfolded.

Not long after I had managed to fall asleep the phone rang, as if the caller was waiting to catch me unaware! It was our landline, which hardly ever rings. I usually keep this phone close to my head and I intentionally have it set to ring loudly in case I am needed for a work emergency. The last thing I was expecting was a call on this phone, and when it rang, I grabbed it and jumped out of bed. Syrsa was still asleep, but I am sure she was just as startled as I was. I left the bedroom quickly to avoid disturbing her further and took the call downstairs. It was my Uncle Riyad from Syria, who I had not seen for almost seven years as I had not been back to Damascus since the start of the civil war, though he and I have kept in touch. He is now in his eighties but is as sharp as ever and our conversations are invariably about religion and life. Looking back at my early childhood, I see it was Uncle Riyad who had the most influence on the way I understood what being a Muslim meant. Never a dull moment with him, but it was typically me who called, and never that early.

As is usual for him, as soon as he was reassured that I was fine, his immediate words were straight from the Holy

Quran. He recited the verse which translates as 'Nothing befalls us except what the Almighty has decreed for us' (9/51). His words of support for me were essentially that I should thank the Lord and stay positive. What my uncle said was not a surprise, but the fact that he was the first person I spoke to that day very much was. I had no idea how he came to know about my stabbing, though I assumed that as soon as my sister found out, it did not take long for the rest of the family to know! I am confident he had already been reassured about the physical aspects of the assault, but he wanted to make sure that emotionally and spiritually I was holding it together. I imagine that he waited all night to give me a call and, bless his soul, he finally thought to himself "Ok, it's 07:00 now in the UK, I can give him a ring". As soon as I put the phone down, I noticed something totally unexpected; my neck pain had improved dramatically. I realised that since I had jumped out of bed and started moving, my neck pain had begun to ease. It was the most amazing thing. Just from the fact that I moved and was distracted, that agonising pain settled, albeit temporarily. I got the message and decided that there was no comfort to be gained from going back to bed.

Even though physically I felt exhausted, emotionally I was calm and steady. Speaking to my uncle was probably the best thing I could have asked for to make sure my feelings and thoughts were exactly where I wanted them to be. I got my computer and, as promised, I made an online donation. I closed the computer and felt somewhat pleased with myself that I had kept my promise. I think I then made myself a coffee and got changed. By that point both Syrsa and Ahmad were awake and getting ready for the school drop off which is normally around 08:30. It must have been the third week back at school and, typically with Ahmad, it was the usual last-minute rush. It started to feel like a typical Monday morning. That is, until Syrsa opened the front door.

A man was standing at our doorstep just about to ring the bell, and a few cars were parked outside our house. He introduced himself as a reporter from the *Manchester Evening News*. At least I am sure he introduced himself but, in the rush, Syrsa simply got in the car with Ahmad and off they went leaving me to welcome him. Somehow it didn't feel awkward meeting a reporter early that morning, probably because he appeared pleasant and soft-mannered. I invited him in just as Syrsa was reversing out of the driveway. She later told me that when she saw him going in, she felt uncomfortable that I was left alone with this strange man! Well, I wasn't totally alone; Oaiss was still fast asleep upstairs. Syrsa immediately phoned our dear friend Saima Alvi asking for her help and advice. Sister Saima, as she is normally called, has been a very close friend for years. She runs the school at our Islamic centre in the fashion of a commanding headmistress, but behind the imposing front is a hardworking, lovely and caring person. She is very active in the community, very supportive and very much 'switched on'. Critical to that morning was the fact that Saima was familiar with the media, having recently featured in the TV show My Week as a Muslim, where a white English woman tried to experience what it was like to be a Muslim in the UK. The woman altered her appearance by having her skin tanned and by wearing the Islamic head scarf, the hijab. It was a fascinating documentary that Syrsa and I thoroughly enjoyed.

Shortly after Syrsa returned, Saima also arrived having dropped off her children at school as well. By then, things started to get a bit chaotic as more reporters were showing up at the front door. A BBC reporter phoned to request attending at about 10:00, but others simply showed up. Syrsa and Saima were agitated; they both shared the worry that I should not engage with the media so early on. They were concerned that the circumstances of the crime might be exploited or misrepresented. They were also worried that I might not have been in the best frame of mind to be interviewed as I had not had any chance to prepare, to consider what I might say. To make matters worse, we received confirmation from the police that my statement was to be taken at 13:00 at Altrincham Police Station, and the advice the officer gave over the phone was to not engage with the media as it risked affecting future legal proceedings. Everyone was asking me to not engage with the media, but somehow none of that mattered to me at the time. I just felt very much at ease. I didn't feel intimidated by the media's presence, nor by the request from the police. To be fair, what the police were concerned about was me providing details of the attack to the media before I submitted my formal statement, and this was very sensible especially considering how I might have interpreted the reason for the crime, for example, and what the attacker had said to me. In addition to possible legal implications, there was also potential for inflaming an already delicate situation. To their credit, the reporters who attended that day were very professional and reassured me that they were fully aware of the rules and limitations of their remit pending submission of my formal statement. They confirmed that even if I inadvertently mentioned something that was 'out of remit', it would not be broadcasted until such information had been made public by the police. For that reason, their questioning was going to be more about how I felt and less about details. The nature of this dialogue may well have played a part in how I presented my sense of forgiveness that morning, because as well as instinctively reflecting on how I felt, I was being asked to discuss it, to present it.

I am not sure, but I assume that the reporters who came to our house that morning may have been slightly surprised by how calm and normal the atmosphere was. Oddly enough, the only thing that was unusual was their presence! This unexpected intrusion could have been overwhelming for us if it wasn't for Saima, and later her sister who also came over; both were able to manage the evolving chaos. Throughout the morning I was receiving messages of support and I remember receiving a call from Bishop Clark, a close friend for many years, and I am sure I was overheard saying to him "God has been very merciful to me". I cannot explain it, but despite the mayhem at our home, I appeared to be calm, though by now I was also buzzing on the inside. I felt alert and very perceptive of what was going on around me. I may have appeared at ease, but I was not in a passive mood. Surprisingly, sensing the anxiety of both Syrsa and Saima made me feel the more relaxed as I left them to worry on my behalf!

By then, the *Manchester Evening News* cameraman had arrived, and we agreed to start their interview in our conservatory. It is safe to say that I have never before been interviewed by the media. Pat Hurst, a pleasant and soft-spoken man from the *Manchester Evening News*, had been the first reporter to show up at our doorstep, so he had the first interview, and considering the evolving mayhem that morning, he helped me feel quite comfortable and relaxed. I believe that his being the first to interview me must have played a role in how I articulated my thoughts on forgiveness. During our informal conversation just before the interview he must have sensed my mood and understood somehow what I wanted to say; I wasn't interested in talking about the event itself as much as I was in talking about how I felt that morning. His line of questioning was very thoughtful, and it is certainly in part to his credit that I was able to articulate my forgiveness. I remain indebted to him for that.

He started by asking me how I was feeling that morning and I think I again said that God had been very merciful to me and I was very grateful and very thankful. Somehow, I then said that I had no hatred, I harboured no anger or any ill feeling towards the person who stabbed me. Out of the blue, Mr Hurst then asked, "So do you forgive him?" Without hesitation I said, "Totally. Absolutely."

There it was. My life-changing moment. At the time, I didn't realise the impact of what I had just said, but within me, I had a sense of immense joy and satisfaction. I felt that my words were true to my deepest feelings, and to how my wife and my children felt. I am grateful to Mr Hurst for his ability to bring this out in the manner he did, for this is likely the moment I will be remembered for. As expected, the section of the interview where I expressed my forgiveness was televised locally, but to my surprise it quickly gained national and international attention. The previous night, the news was fast attracting fear, anger and resentment. But the following day, the news of forgiveness emerged and immediately put an end to all that. The headlines changed and with them so did the public mood. Even though my expression of forgiveness was very personal, I am still amazed as how powerful it also was for others.

Nevertheless, as soon as Syrsa realised the interviews were being videoed, her immediate concern was that I should have had my hair brushed, and as expected, she did not approve of the shirt I had chosen to wear. In a strange sense, as a family we were getting quickly back to normal! Ahmad went to school that Monday morning when, probably, and reasonably, it would have been expected he might miss a few days to get over such a traumatic event. However, at school he didn't show any signs that he was troubled or traumatised. This was also the case for Assma and Oaiss. Very early on, I thereby started to appreciate the immense power of forgiveness. I honestly believe that of all the things that have shaped my life, my expression of forgiveness that morning was the most significant for me.

I think the next interview I had was with the BBC reporter. By then, the house was getting more crowded and there was less time to get to know those who were about to interview me. The second interview felt somewhat impersonal, simply exploring the facts of the stabbing, but by then I was comfortable doing that. I'm not entirely sure when, but at some stage I was asked to consider why I thought that I, in particular, had been targeted. I distinctly recall that I had to pause and think 'Why me?' and I realised that I was no longer responding instinctively. In fact, it was not something that I had given much thought to or even wanted to explore just yet. For some reason I didn't feel comfortable addressing that line of questioning, but I wasn't entirely sure why I felt that way. One possible reason is how I viewed faith, and my relationship with God. In all faiths there is a hierarchy of what is important, and the question "Why me?" in a rhetorical sense just never came to mind. Another possible reason was the fact that I simply did not know "Why me?", and I was not prepared to make up an answer. However, as I started considering the issue, I sensed a conflict within me and very soon, I realised I was not alone in having such a conflict.

The question "Why me?" was not just mine to consider, as there was a real possibility that this had been a hate crime, even possibly a terrorist attack. The news the previous night was already provocative. It started to dawn on me that the question of why I had been attacked had wider implications, and as the only witness to my crime, avoiding the question was not an option. At a community level, the possibility that this was a far-right hate attack had already created an atmosphere of fear. This wasn't the first time my community had been threatened by the far right, but previously these threats never escalated to physical violence of this nature. On a wider scale, such a possibility had already started to swell anger and resentment within the Muslim communities with real potential for escalation. It did not take me long to realise that I could not escape the responsibility of this question and that I had to be honest, fair and objective.

Later that morning I was interviewed by ITV. By then, we moved into our living room where the ITV crew set up lighting and a camera, and I had a different shirt on! The question of why I thought I had been targeted came up again. All I could bring myself to say was that I was not attacked for the watch I was wearing or for the money in my pocket. This was as much as I could say without insinuating a motive. I was being careful with the words I used and avoiding expressing anger or hate. What I said was in fact truthful, and I aimed for it to not stray too far into suggesting a motive. I was sure that my stabbing was not part of a violent robbery; it was simply a violent attack. When I was attacked, the young man wanted to harm me and nothing else. There was no warning, and he demanded nothing of me. He simply snuck up behind me and stabbed me in the neck. When he realised I was still standing, he ran after me. I knew I was petrified, and I knew he wanted to harm me. What I did not know was why he wanted to cause me such serious harm. Nevertheless, I was being asked to suggest a reason. Looking back at that morning, I am very proud of myself that I was not tempted at any time to accuse my attacker with my own assumptions. I believe that it was also during the ITV interview that I mentioned what I thought the attacker shouted at me, "This is for what you've done".

That morning, I started to appreciate how easy it is to make assumptions and how readily people are prepared to believe them, especially when they are uttered by a victim. But very early on I didn't feel or behave typically as a victim. I do not know why this was the case, but I think that the events and emotions that led me to forgive also dispelled feelings of victimisation. I believe that because I did not see myself as a victim, this allowed me to be true to myself and true to my faith. Faith is very much about fairness. You have to be fair to everybody, including a person who intends or intended to harm you. This means that you have to try your utmost to be honest, objective and non-judgmental and to refrain from putting words in their mouth as well as from assuming or suggesting intentions regarding their actions. To do otherwise would be unfair. There was no dilemma in my mind; if I truly believe in God's will, how could I respond by being unfair? To this day, I have never doubted or regretted what happened that morning. The only thing that I cannot really work out is how the hell I managed to do it.

The response to this forgiveness was overwhelming. Over the following few days I received hundreds of supportive messages and it was somehow therapeutic reading and responding to each and every one. The warmth that I felt from total strangers telling me how they were moved by my response had a very significant impact on me. It was very emotional for me on many levels but one of the unexpected feelings was that I felt a sense of belonging. I still find it difficult to express all the feelings that I had, but probably the best way I can describe this is that I felt a deep sense of inner comfort. I remember I was very happy with myself and I did not want this feeling to stop. It is not my habit to seek approval for my actions, but when the messages started to come it was amazing.

There were, however, a few dissenting voices. Even though they conceded that my hasty forgiveness was admirable, to them it was also naïve and a possible betrayal. It was as if my forgiveness had somehow excused the actions of my attacker and undermined or even condoned the harms of extremism and Islamophobia. Even before the true nature of the attack was revealed, there needed to be a louder expression of pain, of anger and of fear; anything to exploit the narratives of anger and hate. To express a feeling of gratitude, to be forgiving and to have a smile on my face so early on was viewed by a small minority as naïve and an expression of weakness. I must admit that there were moments, though they were few, when I questioned myself. I needed to be true to myself and part of that was the need to question if what I did was indeed naïve or an act of betrayal.

The interviews which took place that morning and the subsequent responses set the tone for what was to come, which was dealing with the perception that this may have been a hate crime. This was difficult for me and far removed from any deep sense of inner comfort. Even though I was not comfortable with the dissenting voices, I felt that it was becoming my responsibility to address them. On reflection, I feel that my forgiveness and the fact that I did not feel to be straightforwardly a victim also allowed me to listen to the dissenting voices in an objective manner and to see beyond the negative emotions, though this was not easy. These voices helped me start to consider the issues of hate crimes and extremism and to consider if as a Muslim my case would be dealt with in any particular way, but I was able to do all this thinking relatively objectively. I cannot stress how important this was for me as I quickly realised that it is very easy to lose or even disregard objectivity when emotions are running high.

Nevertheless, and almost unwittingly, I was becoming involved in the issue of 'hate crime', something that I never considered before, and honestly felt even then that I simply did not have the time for. It was not surprising that my story started to attract interest from organisations that tackled discrimination and hate, and they wanted me to be involved. One of the first to approach me within the week was Faith Matters. I owe it to them for raising my awareness and for sparking my interest in countering 'hate'. I knew early on that I wanted to be involved, but I had no clue where I would fit. However, being in the company of such activists, I quickly realised that my knowledge was at best rudimentary, so I needed to get up to speed. Over the next few weeks, I started reading everything and anything to do with racist and hate-related incidents and crimes, the relevant Criminal Acts governing these offences as well as the responsibilities of the police and the CPS. Inevitably I came across the Stephen Lawrence case and many similar cases that exposed institutional racism.

This was very difficult reading, because in the midst of all this was my own case. I had to understand and deal with what the police and the CPS did, as well as the public's response to the investigation and the charge against my attacker, especially the perception that my forgiveness may influence the outcome. This was not easy for me as I was still no more than a few days on from almost being killed and my priority was to get my life back on track. Now that I reflect back on that morning with some distance, I honestly believe

that harbouring no hate, resentment or anger against my
attacker was what changed my life. My faith, my family, my
community and my work have shaped my character to be
able to feel that way so early on, and I am forever grateful for
all of that. But there was also the moment of forgiveness,
alone. I can only say that there are moments in our lives, very
few moments, where we can make a difference, and without
exception, honesty, truthfulness, is key to such moments.
That morning, when I expressed my forgiveness, I can at least
be confident in saying that I was true to everything that had
shaped me.

Chapter 5

"Did you feel he wanted to kill you?"

My interview with the police was scheduled for around 13:30. Fortunately, one of my friends managed to bring my car home from where it was parked the previous evening. My intention was to provide my statement and then head off to work straight after that. I wanted to return to work as soon as possible, but first I needed to make sure I could drive safely. I sat in my car, opened the windows and gently tested my neck. I would turn my head to one side as much as I could tolerate, hold it for a few seconds and then turn in the opposite direction and do the same. As I started, the pain was horrendous, but I kept this going for a few minutes until eventually I was able to turn my head enough to see behind my shoulders, by which time the pain was tolerable. I had taken another little step to my recovery and I was somewhat pleased with myself. I figured out early on that to recover I needed to keep moving, so resting was a waste of time.

Earlier that morning, the police gave me an option of either providing a written or a video statement. I had no clue what either meant, though it was suggested that when we eventually got to court, a video format would potentially present a more powerful personal account rather than simply a written statement. It was explained to me that the video allows the jury to see the victim as a person; they would hear his voice, see his face, his emotions, things that a written statement can never show. I felt comfortable with the idea as I also understood that the video recording would be transcribed as a matter of routine and would be presented as a written statement as well. There was, however, a minor glitch; my local police station in Altrincham did not have the necessary equipment. This would have to be sent over from another station and would need to be set up and tested before the interview, causing a delay. A larger connected problem was that the interview team needed to be familiar with the equipment, and I was left with the impression that the officers who subsequently took my statement, though they could operate the recording equipment, were probably not the most experienced in dealing with a crime such as mine. I believe I was told that their expertise was in child-related offences. Nonetheless, they were able to conduct the interview and obtain a good audio-visual recording, though it never made its way to court!

That afternoon, Saima insisted on attending the interview with me, which made me slightly uncomfortable, but I am sure this was at Syrsa's instructions. Truthfully, I didn't know what to expect, but once we entered the police station, Saima's presence was comforting. Walking through the station, all the corridors looked much the same, with doors slamming shut behind as I would turn into another featureless corridor. It didn't take long before I lost orientation. I am not sure why, but throughout that experience, I just did not feel I was part of the process. I knew that everyone present, including myself, was there for an important procedure, but it did not feel that we were there for me. The officers appeared young, even younger than some of my trainees, which instinctively made me feel responsible for them. Saima's presence, however, provided a different perspective. Throughout our quick tour of the station, she was questioning things and demanding to know what was going on. I honestly thought that at some point they were going to call it a day and throw both of us out. I felt a bit unsettled and decided to play it safe and keep my mouth shut. The last thing I wanted to do was to appear intimidating in a police station!

Later on, I came to realise that the provision of my statement that afternoon was to be my only input to the entire legal proceeding. Beyond that, my voice was no longer necessary or relevant, and this was something I regretted in the months to come, as that afternoon I felt I let myself down. On further reflection, however, I don't think I could have acted any differently. In my state of mind at the time, I could not have been inquisitive or critical. I simply put my trust in the hands of these professionals, these officers. I am sure that is what my patients do when they come to see me. However, I recall that Saima was trying to be my advocate, presenting a perspective that I simply lacked. I heard her saying to one of the officers: "You do realise this is a serious crime?", "Do you realise he could have been killed?", "Are you sure you are doing everything right?" As I listened to her, I was thinking, "Saima, what the hell are you trying to do?". I honestly thought anytime now they will just ask us to leave, and really, do you need to be reminding me that I could have died last night? It just felt horribly funny, and I did have a laugh about this with Syrsa later. However, now that I have experienced more of the criminal justice system, I realise how important one question was: "Do you realise he could have been killed?" I will return to this question.

This may sound odd, but I could not help the sense that as I answered the interview questions, I felt as if I were sitting an exam. It could just be a habit, but I was very focused on getting the answers right and making sure I didn't miss anything out. I did not want to let the process, or myself, down. Unfortunately, when you concentrate on answering, you do not leave much room for questioning the broader context of those questions. Though how would I know what the questions in a stabbing case should be? In my interview, they were after hard facts. I was asked about things like distances, height, time, this and that etc. There was no mention of how I felt, what it was like being chased, or how petrified I was. At some point, I felt as if they were quizzing me on technical details to make sure I wasn't fabricating a story. At no time was there any mention of or reference to the fact that I could have been killed in this attack. It was a few weeks later that the question dawned on me; did the police really believe that I was actually violently stabbed and could have been killed? All the police had was an alleged crime, no witnesses, a five-centimetre cut, and a victim that was discharged the same evening from hospital and who was already walking and driving in less than 24 hours. I spent a few nights questioning if my determination to get back on my feet so quickly may have undermined the seriousness of what had taken place; what a horrible thought!

It was only much later, after the trial was over, that I fully understood the relevance of what took place that day of the interview. Knowing that I was the only witness to my crime, it essentially boiled down to my word against that of my attacker. When I said that he shouted at me "This is for what you've done", the police simply did not believe me, and why should they? I know full well that their scepticism was not personal, it had nothing to do with who I am. It was simply about the fairness that the judicial system must afford the defendant, which is something that I support wholeheartedly. I eventually concluded that the victim cannot be trusted to give an unbiased account of a crime. Unless there are witnesses, the victim's account is invariably second to that of the defendant. It would be unfair otherwise.

Relatedly, on the day of the attack shortly after I had been rushed to hospital, there was some kind of a melee gathering outside our centre. To their credit, the police noticed a man behaving in a distinctly odd manner. On questioning, they became suspicious of this character and apprehended him. It quickly transpired that this young man was related to my attacker and within the hour, the police were in the process of arresting the young man who stabbed me, and a large kitchen knife was retrieved. This was nothing short of a fantastic piece of brilliant policing. During the trial, I watched the bodycam videos of the arrest that took place that evening and I could hear my attacker ranting about how he wanted to stab and kill someone. He gave a frank and blatant account that was recorded by the arresting officers. In effect, the police had the case in the bag within the hour, before I had even left the hospital. They had the attacker, they had an unsolicited confession, and they had the weapon. To all intents and purposes, it was done and dusted, but they needed to go through the rest of their procedures, which included my statement. Knowing what had taken place the previous evening, it is not surprising that my statement was a simple routine of dotting the i's and crossing the t's.

When I went home after giving my statement, Saima's sister, Aisha, who is a barrister, wanted to know if the police had asked me whether I had been afraid for my life? "Did they ask you if you felt he wanted to kill you?" I said "No, nothing of the sort". I saw the frustration on her face, but I wasn't sure what she was talking about. It did not take long to realise that in this process you do not get a second chance. Once the interview is done, you're done. I told Aisha they wanted specific details like "How many cars were there between me and him?", "What was the distance?", "How far did I walk into the mosque?". Yet during the trial, these details were of absolutely no material value whatsoever. When it came to my day in court, I couldn't help but think that not only was my video statement a total waste of time, but it may have even detracted from what had taken place. I later concluded that once the defendant was arrested, the investigation into my stabbing was also arrested, as it were. I recall that before leaving the station, I asked one of the officers if he wanted to take a picture of my neck and the wound as evidence. He looked surprised being asked such a question, but the answer was "No"; it was apparently not necessary.

Looking back, I can see that everything I said in the interview was simply to verify what the police already knew, and in all honesty, I am not comfortable with that. A decision had already been made, and my input was no longer material to the process: it was no longer relevant as to where in my neck I was stabbed; it was no longer relevant how deep the knife had penetrated and how close I came to being killed; it was no longer relevant why I was the victim. It is very awkward when you come to realise that you are being patronised in a process that you feel you ought to be central to. However, being the person I am, I realise that fairness dictates I need to step into the other's shoes. How else could the police have managed my incident, given the fact that they had the attacker, his confession and the weapon within the hour? I have to accept that for legal reasons, the police are very restricted in what they could share with me. Should the case go to court, the slightest error could be very costly to everyone involved. Indeed, the judicial system is at its fairest to the victim when the police carry out their duty diligently. To the public, the victim is the centre of attention. But to the criminal justice system, it is the defendant. It took me some time to come to terms with this critical distinction, but my forgiveness allowed me to accept it without feeling angry or resentful. Nevertheless, this all opened my eyes to the fact that within the criminal justice system there is no meaningful dialogue with the victim beyond their statement. I was offered support, but this was to deal with the "ordeal of this violent encounter". Gladly, this was something I did not need. Later, we were allocated a very thoughtful and understanding support officer. But what I needed on that day was an advocate that made me feel that I meant something to a process I was part of, an advocate who would make sure that the right questions were asked, and that I also had a chance to ask legitimate questions relevant to me, that my voice was at least on the same standing as that of the person who nearly killed me. I still wonder if I had been asked whether I felt he had wanted to kill me, whether that would have made a difference. I am not sure it would.

Chapter 6

Don't You Dare Look Back

The recording of my police statement took longer than I anticipated, and I needed to head off to my clinic quickly. I remember, though, that as I hurried to my car, I was approached by a young man who had been waiting for me on his own in the car park. It was an odd impromptu encounter, but he quickly showed me his ID and introduced himself as a reporter from one of the local radio stations. I have a vague memory of his face and his colourful jumper, but I distinctly recall his handheld recorder with an orange microphone foam cover. I gave a quick interview, but I think if it wasn't for that nostalgic orange foam cover, I would probably have made an excuse to leave. I sat in the car, got my neck moving again and rang the hospital to let them know I was on my way. I am glad I did so as it turned out they had already cancelled my clinic, assuming I would not be working that day! I must admit I felt somewhat deflated as planning to get to my clinic that afternoon had been an important motivator for me. I may have been unrealistic, setting myself that target, but cancelling the clinic was one of many decisions that would be taken on my behalf in the coming few days, which was something I struggled with. In this case, though, and even though I was disappointed, it was the right decision. I had not had much sleep, the day had been exhausting, and the pain had started to kick in. By now it was almost 24 hours since I had been stabbed, and it finally felt like it was catching up with me. I was also relieved to call it a day.

It was probably naïve of me to think it was going to be that simple. By the time I arrived home, it seems that one of my earlier interviews had already been on the national news. As soon as I entered, Ahmad shouted, "Dad, you've been on TV!" and he showed me a short recording he took on his phone. He must have had a shock when he saw his dad on TV and just managed to get his phone in time to record the last few seconds. All of a sudden, I wasn't as deflated. I was eager to see the whole recording, but I had to wait for the next news bulletin. It wasn't long before the six o'clock news came on and we all sat watching, waiting for my news report. It sounds odd, but when it came to my story, even though I felt excited, I also felt awkward watching and listening to myself and to my story. The clip lasted less than a minute and it was done! I wanted to see more, but that was it. It finished far too quickly for me; this was my first introduction to the power of editing. Earlier in the day the ITV interview lasted probably 15 minutes and everything I said was very important to me. To be honest, during the interview, I got a sense that I had an important story to tell. The reporter was very clever in creating that feeling and in getting me in the mood to engage and to speak from my heart. For me, that evening, naïvely again, I really wanted to see my whole interview. This was, and still is, an unfulfilled wish.

Shortly after the news, I went back to the small room by the kitchen. I was still in my own little world, unaware of what was unfolding beyond. I just don't think I was ready to engage with all that just yet. I instinctively felt a need to look inwards and to focus on personal goals to get my life back on track. I probably appeared to be selfish, but my immediate priority was for everyone at home to get back to our routine and for me to get back to work. I honestly don't think I could have been able to do that while engaging with everything else that was going on. There was, however, a price to pay for all this focus on myself and immediate family as decisions were already being made on my behalf, seemingly in my best interests, but without me involved. I started to realise that I needed to get out of my bubble, and quickly. Events were unfolding without me. In the community meeting that took place the previous evening, for example, the police had announced their decision to classify my stabbing as a hate crime. Further discussions that took place in that meeting were designed to reassure the community, but they were never officially shared with me. Also, the fact that my attacker had been arrested so quickly proved significant as it allowed for the incident to be rapidly de-escalated and the police were able to rule out the possibility of a terrorist attack. Very early, the police satisfied themselves that this was not an organised attack by an extremist group or individual. However, I later became aware that during that evening meeting, it became apparent the police were not up to date with the far-right activity in our area, which was a focus that became very important to me in the months to come. So, even though this meeting became about more than only my stabbing, I still find it disappointing that its contents were not officially shared with me. For whatever reason, there seems to be an unwritten law that victims of violent crime should not be involved beyond the violence they had suffered.

That Monday evening, a vigil was organised in partnership with the 'We Stand Together' campaign. This turned out to be a wonderful initiative as it helped my community and my neighbourhood start to recover from this ordeal. My stabbing may have been an isolated personal incident, but where it took place and who the victim was gave it a more significant public perspective. My Muslim community felt vulnerable and threatened. Our elderly neighbours on Grove Lane who have lived next to the Islamic centre for many years were very frightened as they have never witnessed such violence on their doorstep. The close-knit Altrincham interfaith community was shocked and dismayed by such senseless violence, but more importantly, they felt that the Muslim community needed them by their side. Despite the very short notice, the call to the vigil had an overwhelming response with over 200 people attending, including friends from our local synagogues, local churches and other faith communities. There were local dignitaries, councillors, as well as representatives from local schools and the police. Sadly, I missed the vigil and all I have in memory is a picture of the back hall packed with people and a picture of friends holding a 'We Stand Together' banner. I can only imagine what the emotions running through everyone were like that evening as the community was trying to get a sense of what had happened and how best to respond.

Looking back at those early days I am very happy I did not add fuel to these emotions, and it was probably right that I stayed at home that evening. However, this wasn't only my decision. Since my afternoon clinic was cancelled, I told Syrsa I was considering attending the vigil, but she quickly put some sense into me! I remember her telling me I looked exhausted, and she questioned if it was necessary for me to be there. I, of course, willingly conceded. It had already been a long and eventful day and it made sense that we should have an early night. We were all tired, but we also felt content and happy; the first day had passed. Other than a few phone calls, I spent the rest of the evening going through my messages. I hate to admit it, but, other than WhatsApp, I am pretty much useless with other social media platforms. I am sure I had Facebook and Twitter accounts then, but I hardly ever used them; probably I never felt comfortable enough to do so. It was thanks to Oaiss who kept sharing with me people's comments on social media, and I remember how excited he was. That evening, it was very obvious that the mood had changed completely. Within a day, there was no more anger about the stabbing; it was all about forgiveness. The angry and hateful messages stopped abruptly and completely. I remember feeling very happy that night and at last I was able to have a good night's sleep. I am not sure, and this may sound silly, but I honestly think that feeling happy that night made my neck pain feel much easier and it did not take me long to dose off.

Tuesday turned out to be one of the most amazing days of my life. My normal Tuesday routine is to be up at 07:00 and be at work by 08:00 to start my pre-operative ward round and preparations. The rest of the day is then spent in the operating theatre, usually finishing by 17:00. It is a good day's work, and this has been my Tuesday routine for years. For that day, my operating list was cancelled as it was not certain whether I would have been able to cope physically and mentally through the demands of a full day's operating. Everyone at work assumed that I would be staying at home! I must confess I did have a slight lie-in that morning. By the time I woke up, Syrsa had already dropped Ahmad off at school, so we had breakfast together. There was no one at our doorstep and there were no more cars parked beside our drive. Apart from having breakfast there was nothing unusual about that morning, but that was soon to change. Even though my operating list had been cancelled, I needed to be back at work. The previous week I had been on study leave attending the annual National Orthopaedic conference, which meant the usual few hundred emails and a week's worth of paperwork to get back to. This week was also special as for the past three months we had been preparing for our first 'simulation human factors' training day. As it happened, the training was set for Thursday with patient actors, surgical teams and theatre staff already registered for the event. My stabbing could not have happened at a more inconvenient time. I had already earmarked Monday to finalise the preparations and I was getting anxious that all this hard work could go to waste. Thankfully, cancelling my operative list gave me a chance to catch up, and there was no time to waste.

I got myself ready as usual, got in the car and drove to work, and because I arrived late, I ended up having to park at the far end of the car park as it was packed by then. On Google Maps, our staff car park is officially named Jurassic as in addition to the high fencing and exposure to the elements, the terrain at the far end can be described as adventurous and remains alien to tarmac. By the time I arrived the car park was relatively empty of people and as I walked across everything appeared to be usual. But a few minutes later I went through entrance 15 and suddenly, everything became very unusual. As I walked along the corridor, I realised that everyone was looking at me. It was very strange. It felt odd but equally pleasant and I just carried on walking. The same thing kept happening. It started with a glance, and then a person's eyes opened wider and, for that second or two, I could see shock. The next person's eyes would then light up and then the next. I acknowledged each with a smile and a nod. Hospital corridors are typically very long, but that morning I didn't mind that at all. These looks I was getting were not just from people I knew, they were from everyone: porters, cleaners, nurses, people that normally would perhaps just pass me by every morning with everyone minding their own business. That morning, everyone had a smile on their face, and now and again someone would spontaneously say "Good on you", or "Well done", things like that. The best way I can sum up my feelings that morning were joy and humility. I felt they were happy for me and for what I did, and they wanted to share it with me. It was all wonderfully spontaneous, which was particularly striking because typically when it comes to a hospital consultant, there is an air of formality. That morning, it was all spontaneous and everyone was being themselves, even if it was just for those few seconds. It was amazing. I felt as if I was floating on my way to my office. As I arrived at my department, one of the nurses rushed up to me and joked "I could have thought of some consultants that deserved stabbing, but not you!" It is funny how people express the unjustness of life. She had a big smile on her face, but her eyes and voice could not hide the shock. She was consoling me in her own way. That morning, everyone was genuine. I felt their happiness that I was alive and recovering and that I was there, back at work. I also felt from them a sense of pride that I was one of them. The good feeling that morning was simply wonderful.

By the time I arrived at my office, I started to realise more of what my forgiveness meant to others. The happiness expressed by everyone was genuine and impulsive, probably reflecting the fact that it was so soon after the stabbing and everyone was still living with their early, honest emotions. What was even more amazing was when I entered my secretary's office and said good morning. There were six secretaries sitting there, and all I could see was six faces looking at me, astonished and silent. I stood there for a couple of seconds, but they still appeared stunned. I went to my office down the corridor, got some papers, came back, and opened the door. The same reaction! No words, nothing, they just turned around and looked at me, still silent. Not a word. I thought to myself "I had better get used to this".

I went back to my office and started going through emails. A few minutes later one of my consultant colleagues walked in, sat down, and started crying. She then spoke her heart. She told me how glad she was that I was there, how shocked she was when she found out I was stabbed and that she couldn't sleep and had been crying all night. Suddenly there I was consoling her, helping her cope with the trauma that she went through from knowing a close colleague of hers was stabbed. It soon hit me that those closest to me at work have themselves been through an ordeal in that one of their colleagues could have been killed. I realised that as the victim of a violent crime I had a role in consoling and reassuring those who are close to me, who had also been affected. Returning to work that morning was so important not just for me, but for those close to me as well, and being there for my colleagues lifted me up tremendously. Another colleague came in and told me that until I had replied to an SMS she had sent me that evening, letting her know I was OK, she had been beside herself. Other colleagues came in and expressed themselves, each in their own way, all amazing.

When I returned later to the secretaries' office, they manged to snap out of their stunned state. My secretary asked me if I could spare a couple of minutes. They sat me down and told me "You're not going to move". They all went out and came back with boxes of chocolates and a card, which they had ready for me. They tried to tell me how they felt but it was obvious they were still shocked. For me it was not necessary for them to say anything. I knew how they felt, and it was a much-needed wonderful expression of support.

With all this going on, I was naturally feeling extremely good about myself. That morning was very intense, but I could see that even though my presence was important, I also realised that I could be a distraction. I decided to stick to my office for the rest of the day and get through my admin work. As I went through emails, many of which were wishing me well, I was taken aback by a message from our medical director. It was thoughtful and from the heart. She wrote that she had been moved by what I said on the news, and she said something along the lines of even though she did not herself have a strong belief in a creator, she believed that someone was looking after me that day. As I went through the many wonderful messages, there was no doubt that everyone was utterly shocked by the senseless violence and they were delighted I walked away from such a severe attack. But the thing that touched me most was how moved my colleagues were by my forgiveness. The change in mood over the past 24 hours made me realise that there is something magical about forgiveness. It wasn't just about feeling happy, but I sensed that it was about giving a sense of hope. Even though many colleagues openly expressed the fact that they would not have been able to forgive such a person, they were very glad that I felt able to do so.

Still at my desk, I gradually started to get into some rhythm of work. However, I had noticed early on that my ability to concentrate was not as it should be. I wasn't sure if that was just me coming back from a week's leave or it was the effect of the stabbing. I spoke to my medical director and suggested that from a safety point of view, it would be appropriate for me to have a mental-health assessment. I needed to make sure that I was not carrying any psychological trauma and, most importantly, I needed to make sure I was ready and safe to treat patients. Fortunately, an assessment was quickly arranged for the following morning. I then decided to stay on that afternoon to see if I had the stamina for a full day's work. It was a bit of a struggle, but I was able to stick it out until 17:30 before heading home.

Walking along the same corridors back to my car was not as dramatic as it had been in the morning. Then as I entered Jurassic, I realised that the car park was now almost empty, especially towards the far end, and at some stage I noticed I was walking alone. I don't know why, but I started to get an uncomfortable sense of who might be behind me. The feeling came out of the blue and I felt frightened, but also stupid. When I was attacked, I was alone, and the young man snuck up behind me; there had been no sound, no warning, nothing. As I walked across Jurassic, I started to look behind me but as I was about to turn my head, I implored myself "Don't be stupid, there is nobody behind you. Don't you dare look back. What really are the chances that someone is going to sneak up behind you with a knife, again?" I just kept walking and telling myself that if I looked back, I was an idiot. I carried on walking and reassuring myself, and I didn't look back. I refused to do so until I got to my car. It was a difficult dialogue with myself because I was frightened and my heart was pounding, but as I sat in my car, it was over, and I have never had that feeling again. I believe Mark Twain once said that courage is not merely the absence of fear; nobody can simply choose to not be afraid, but it is what you do with your fear that matters. On reflection, I am glad that I ended up parking where I did that morning and that I was alone when I walked back. It gave me the chance to face a fear that I had not anticipated, and I felt I had taken a massive step in my recovery.

That evening I was due to have an interview with the Canadian organisation CBC News. By the time the interview came around I had heard that the person who had been arrested had been charged, and that he was charged with

Section 18 and possession of an offensive weapon. I did not know at the time what Section 18 meant, but there was no mention of attempted murder and no mention of the attack being a hate crime. Much of the CBC interview was fine, but at one point I was asked "Why did they not charge him with hate?" and for the first time since the attack, I was lost for words. I did not have an instinctive answer and I did not have a rational answer either. I simply could not answer the question, and I remained silent. A couple of seconds passed before the interviewer intervened and said, "I believe during the incident the attacker had said "This is for what you've done", and I said "Yes". She then joked saying "Perhaps the attacker had meant because you were a doctor?" She was openly mocking the idea that this was some random attack, and clearly also she was mocking the charge. She was reinforcing what I already sensed from some of my friends, that since I am a Muslim the wheels of justice will somehow be turned differently. For the first time I was having to publicly face up to issues of Islamophobia and hate crime. It was far too early for me to deal with these, and I felt uncomfortable and, interestingly, I felt my neck pain was getting worse. This again may sound silly, but for the three years since the stabbing, whenever I have had negative thoughts about my attack, I feel a deep pain where I was stabbed. I had many good reasons to stay positive and probably avoiding pain was just as good as any, but within just two days of the stabbing I was having to address issues relating to the criminal justice system and hate-crime legislation. I also felt that I was being encouraged to give an opinion based on my feelings rather than hard facts. The long and short of it was that I was not prepared. I needed information and I needed help. This was the second time I felt I needed an advocate.

In my basic understanding, I had simply assumed that the police would have charged the person with committing a hate crime, and I had assumed from my clinical background that wilfully stabbing someone in the neck would be considered as attempted murder. When the charge was announced, I was having to answer why this particular charge was made, as if I could have an answer. However, I did realise early on that I had a responsibility to face up to these questions. I just felt that at two days, it was far too soon for me to take all this on. I did, though, quickly realise that I did not have the luxury of time. I must admit that after an amazing start to the day, I was now feeling somewhat inadequate and frustrated, which turned out to be just the impetus I needed.

Chapter 7

Section 18

The charge Section 18 is defined as grievous bodily harm (GBH) with intent. It is described as "wounding with intent" or "causing grievous bodily harm with intent", and that issue of "intent" can, perhaps unsurprisingly, be complex. It is defined in law as "the decision to bring about a prohibited consequence", which as I understand it, means committing the act not by accident. It serves the purpose of distinguishing a type of "motivation" from other possibilities such as "recklessness". My alleged attacker was also charged with possession of an offensive weapon. The offensiveness of a weapon is defined as "any article made or adapted for use to cause injury to the person or intended by the person having it with him for such use".

Anyhow, I was not the only person who was confused about these charges. There was a general perception that Section 18 was a let-down. It was a lesser charge than had been expected, that of attempted murder. After all, why would someone plunge a knife into the back of someone else's neck if they did not want them to die? Section 18 just did not carry the same tone as Attempted Murder and social media was again churning out angry messages. Overnight, the mood had turned again. Even the CBC news reporter was sceptical, and she wasn't local. Having put the phone down on that interview, Syrsa and I sat and talked, still cooped up in the same small room where we felt secure and comfortable. But now, we did not feel as comfortable as we had the past two days. Have we let ourselves and our community down? Were we too naïve to think that we were equal in the eyes of the law? Why are we not as angry as everyone else? We started to argue our case together, but we kept on coming back to same conclusion; we have been very fortunate, we do not know the full facts, and somehow, neither of us were angry. Yes, we admitted to each other that we were ignorant, but were we also foolish to be trusting? Why should we not be trusting, and if we do not trust the police, who can we trust? We eventually agreed that we should not engage with these thoughts. What we firmly agreed on is that we really did not know why that young man walked up behind me and stabbed me. I argued for things and Syrsa argued against them. I said, for example, he must have known that he was at the mosque and he must have realised that I was a Muslim walking into the mosque; how else can you explain it? Syrsa refused to accept my argument and said that I testified that the man crossed the road before I even reached the mosque. He did not know me, and I did not overtly look to be a Muslim. She argued that he must have targeted me before considering that I might or might not be a Muslim. I did not feel comfortable with Syrsa's interpretation, but I had to concede that her point of view was stronger than mine. By the end of our argument, we both felt there was no conclusive evidence that this was a hate-motivated crime. The young man himself had not admitted to that and we were not going to assume otherwise. But then I started to wonder why he was not charged with attempted murder. We both agreed we needed to do our own research.

It was still early evening and we started searching online for information on the charges of Section 18 and on attempted murder. It turned out that a conviction for a Section 18 charge can carry a maximum custodial sentence of 25 years, just the same as for attempted murder. We both started to realise that Section 18 was itself a very serious charge, but unfortunately, from the point of view of public perception, it felt like a let-down. Somehow, the charge needed to reflect who the victim was and how much he was loved and respected. Even worse, I later had to deal with dissenting voices suggesting that my forgiveness had enabled this seemingly lesser charge. Syrsa and I needed to make sense of it all. I think we both helped each other to be fair and objective. It was not an easy discussion, but by the end of the day I remember that we both felt comfortable again. We appreciated the strength of emotions that had been expressed out of love and respect for us, but we needed to keep our own emotions in check. The fact that we both felt no anger or resentment towards the young man who stabbed me helped, and we agreed that we both needed to be fair and just to him.

That evening, Syrsa appeared to have more energy than me and she was really getting stuck in. She loves this kind of challenge, digging for information. Not only that, but for her it also seemed to be a race as to who would find the information first. That evening I had no chance, and it was not long before she started telling me what I needed to know. From her quick search, she found out that if someone is stabbed in the chest this automatically brings about a charge of attempted murder. If someone is stabbed in the head, this also automatically brings about a charge of attempted murder. However, if someone is stabbed in the neck it can go either way. She found reports of some people who had been charged with attempted murder after they had stabbed someone in the neck, and others charged with Section 18 for the same kind of attack. We quickly realised that Section 18 is not an unusual charge in my circumstances. In fact, it was actually a more likely charge for a stabbing in the neck. Between the two of us, we started to see the logic in how the criminal justice system worked. We also realised that we needed to help others see it in the same way. This did not prove to be easy, as many people felt genuinely aggrieved at it not being a charge of attempted murder. They kept phoning and asking us things like, "Don't they know you could have been killed?" as if I needed more reminding. Fortunately for us, we were already past that stage.

The one uncomfortable feeling that I had was the possibility that I was letting my community down by being forgiving and understanding. That is, by seemingly playing down what had happened to me, I may have been giving the impression that it is OK to stab a Muslim. This was all the more pertinent as my stabbing took place within a few months of the Manchester Arena atrocity, a period that witnessed an unprecedented rise in Islamophobic hate crime. Despite the pressures that we felt over the weeks to come, both Syrsa and I strongly believed that if there was a time to be forgiving and to be fair, it was such a time. With that, Tuesday came to an end. We had discussed in Arabic, and I remember that our final words were "God will not accept it other than that" (*Allah-ma-byirda-ghair-heik*).

The meeting that had been arranged for me with the Employee Health and Wellbeing Services team was set for 10:00. There were still a few astonished looks as I walked along the corridor to my office that morning, but not as many as the day before. People were starting to calm down, though when I saw the secretaries again, they still had that look of "Is that really you?" Anyhow, seeing the psychology therapist turned out to be one of the best things I did after the attack. I had a deep feeling that I needed to talk my ordeal through with someone, but I hadn't yet realised how important that would prove to be. Speaking to a therapist, someone totally independent, who just wanted to listen to me, gave me the opportunity to explore my mind in a way that was not possible otherwise. It was an opportunity for me to talk about deeply personal issues with no strings attached. Well, probably just one; I needed to know for myself if I was safe to work with patients.

I started by going into detail about the incident; being late for the prayers, noticing someone crossing the road, the sudden pain in my neck, that angry look on his face and then running away as fast as I could. For some reason, I was focusing mainly on the incident. I spoke of how I ran away in a straight line and how I jumped the steps in one go and then reached that glass door that only opened outwards. But then, for the first time since the stabbing, I suddenly remembered; it was then that I realised how petrified I had been. I had no idea why, but those feelings came rushing back. When I was running away, I remember I hadn't felt anything, I didn't feel scared, there was no time to feel, I just instinctively ran. But when I needed to open the glass door, when I stopped, that was when I felt something. I remembered that I tried to look through the frosted glass hoping that there was a table on the other side, that I wanted something I could hide behind, and I remembered in that split second that I feared for my life. Until that point, I had never recalled that particular moment so vividly. Despite the many interviews, the depth of these feelings never surfaced. I had stopped for less than a second, but I only now remembered that the fear that gripped me had been overwhelming and I desperately needed to hide. Amazingly, my mind had suppressed that fear completely and the memory only came back to me in that therapy session. I felt the same pounding in my heart. But then a second incredible realisation came. Having recalled my fear, as I entered the hall and saw the two ladies, that gripping fear vanished completely. It was then that I also realised how fortunate I was that they were there. For some unknown reason, their presence had an immediate and profound impact on me. It started to cross my mind what might have happened to me if the two of them had not been there. It was also then that I recalled the rear hall is usually locked at that time in the afternoon. What would have happened if there was no meeting that afternoon, if the doors were locked? Even though I felt uncomfortable with all my questions, I couldn't help but feel that there was still a lot for me to be grateful for.

Speaking so freely to the therapist proved to be an incredible experience. All that I did and felt at the time of my stabbing was spontaneous. It was only when I reflected on events in this setting that my deeper feelings surfaced. I had never experienced something like this before and I had no idea or warning that this would happen, but I am very grateful that it did. When I tell my story of what happened that Sunday afternoon, I must recognise that I talk about it through my experience of that following Wednesday morning. I went there wanting to know that I was safe to see patients. By the time I left, I realised how happy I was that I had faced my hidden fear and I was comfortable with it. That fear never surfaced again. We did of course also talk about how I would interact with my patients. She asked me questions along the lines of, "When you are next with a patient, will you be able to concentrate on what they're telling you, or will you be distracted with what had happened to you?" Basically, I needed to be sure I was ready to give patients my undivided attention. I instinctively replied by asking what she thought. I knew by then that I felt well in myself, but I needed her professional input. The response I had was very reassuring. She said that I came across very naturally and I did not seem to be struggling psychologically. She did, however, warn me that I needed to be on the lookout for a possible rebound after such a horrific ordeal. I must admit that I felt very pleased with myself and as I walked back to my office, I knew I had taken another step in my recovery. On a funny note, that session reminded me of a Sheldon Cooper remark from the *Big Bang Theory*: "I am not crazy, my mother had me tested!" Following my session that morning, I did use the remark a few times.

I went to my clinic that afternoon and suggested that I should only see a few patients just to test that I could indeed really cope. I quickly realised that the appointments took longer than usual but this wasn't because my mind was drifting away. It was strange, but I was taking longer because I was somewhat excitable. For instance, as I read a patient's letter, my eyes were racing down the page faster than I could read. I realised that I needed to slow down to be able to concentrate. As soon as I realised what was taking place, I was able to have some control, but nevertheless, I could tell that I was not ready for a full clinic just yet. This was a good start, but I still needed to get myself under control. I received great support from my colleagues for that clinic, which meant it was not necessary for it to be cancelled. I know I could not have done the work without their help, for which I am very grateful. I was able to stay the distance until the clinic was finished by 17:00. Three days had passed by and I was happy with myself.

Chapter 8

Close to Death. So What?

Wednesday afternoon was another critical milestone for me. I decided to have a proper look at my scan, but not on my own. It was just something that I felt I needed to do. Once the clinic had finished, I called one of my radiology colleagues and asked him to come and sit with me while we went through the scan. A CT scan is typically hundreds of detailed images that are taken in three perpendicular planes. In a penetrating injury, such a scan is vital when looking for internal bleeding and tissue damage, but it also serves to accurately assess the depth and angle of penetration. When my scan was first examined, it was essentially undertaken to rule out deep-seated bleeding, but now I wanted to see for myself where the knife had been. I don't remember what drove me to look at my scan, but I knew then that I could not let it go, though it wasn't idle curiosity. A knife had been in my neck and the scan must have picked something up.

The two of us sat there and started going through the images. The process is fairly standard and tedious; we carefully look at images in one plane, then another, and another, before repeating the process a few times until a picture starts to emerge. The changes on the scan can be subtle but we gradually started to pick up signs of damage. We first saw little air bubbles that were sucked in by the knife as it ripped first through the skin and then through muscle. It was definitely on the left side and we could see those tiny little air bubbles projecting upwards and forwards but, crucially, they were drifting further to the left away from my spinal cord. We then spotted tiny little areas of bleeding where the knife sliced through muscle but amazingly all the blood vessels were intact. Eventually I was able to define a subtle outline, a silhouette, of the knife where it penetrated my neck. I saw the silhouette tapering to a point just a couple of centimetres from the major vessels that are at the front of my neck. I could now see where the knife came to a halt. Two centimetres to the right was my spinal cord, two centimetres to the front were my jugular vein and carotid artery.

As I looked at the silhouette of the knife it seemed incredible how everything was missed. I saw little blood vessels lying no more than a millimetre or two from the edge of the silhouette. How the hell did the knife miss everything, absolutely everything? As an orthopaedic surgeon, I have reviewed hundreds of scans in my time, and I do recall occasions when I thought that we had a very lucky patient. As I sat there looking at the silhouette, all I was saying under my breath was "Thank you God". But then came the real shock, which was about the 'level' at which I was stabbed. I could see that the air bubbles were at about the same level as my chin. This meant it was a high-level stabbing, probably at the third or fourth cervical level (C3, C4). I started to get the full picture. The knife had entered my neck just left of the midline at the third cervical vertebra and travelled upwards and slightly to the left. The tip of the knife stopped at the level of the second cervical vertebra. It was then that I felt a cold sweat and a shiver. I knew exactly what happened that day. Thankfully, having my colleague next to me helped me get a grip on my emotions and the uncomfortable feeling did not last long.

In the confines of my mind, I thought I had just accomplished a great piece of detective work. For whatever reason, my mind gradually moved away from "Thank you God" to "I have evidence". I was thinking there it is, this young man surely wanted to kill, otherwise why would he stab me up there in my neck? I did not see it at the time, but I was falling into a trap that I had not anticipated; I became overindulgent with the 'evidence' I managed to unearth. I could now see the path of the knife going upwards in my neck. Surely the person who stabbed me knew that this is how to cause maximum harm? Surely, he knew that this stabbing upwards was the only way for the knife to sneak between the neck bones on its way to my spinal cord. I kept on thinking he must have known what he was doing, he must have known. On reflection, I now realise that I was doing exactly what I set out not to do, which was imputing a purpose to his actions.

At some stage during the following weeks, I shared my findings with the police. I don't know how I came across, speaking to them about my scan, but understandably they were somewhat sceptical and probably thought I was being histrionic. This initial rejection only helped to entrench myself further in my own little bubble. I shared my thoughts with Syrsa, but this time I was not backing down. I was sure I was right; I am the expert here! I had tried to convince the police that I was the expert at this sort of thing with over 25 years of experience, but that did not get me far. It seemed that for everyone involved, my injury was just a minor cut that needed no more than four stiches and an early discharge from hospital. They must have thought "How bad could it be?" Knowing now what my scan showed, I recall that these conflicts were things I struggled with very much at the time. I felt I was not being listened to and that my voice did not matter.

On deep and painful reflection, I think I now know why I was struggling, and it was for all the wrong reasons. I am sure it was in large part due to my pride. Having used my intellect and professional skills to unravel a 'mystery' that no one else could, it was a major let-down that no one was interested. I am now sure it must have been my ego; why else did I feel the need to convince anyone? With that said, I don't fully regret my indulgence. In an odd sort of way this unfortunate struggle made me realise just how easy our minds can trap us. It was a tough and humbling lesson to learn at my age.

Nevertheless, those feelings ran deep within me and in my weeks of frustration, I wrote a vivid account as to what would have happened to me if the tip of the knife was just two centimetres to the right. As I look back now, I cringe a bit; was that really necessary? I took it upon myself to explain (or was it to teach?) my case officer what happened when a victim is stabbed in the back of the neck. I thought in my own way I could shed some light on why some neck stabbings can kill while others don't. I convinced myself I was doing something useful. I was wrong; all I did was delay myself from snapping out of this obsession. Anyway, having gone through the effort I might as well share it now, in brief!

In simple terms, the human neck has seven cervical vertebrae which are numbered one to seven from top to bottom. As we move up the neck, the outcome from a cord injury changes dramatically. If the victim is stabbed at the lower end of the neck, injuring the spinal cord at or below the sixth level, this is not a fatal injury. The unfortunate victim is likely to end up paraplegic, suffering paralysis of the legs and some weakness in the arms. They can still manage some independence, depending on how much use they have left in their arms and hands. If the stabbing is at the fifth level the unfortunate victim will be tetraplegic, losing all power in both lower and upper limbs, but they will still be able to support their breathing. This is primarily due to our phrenic nerves which leave the neck from the third to the fifth cervical levels. It is these two nerves, one on either side, which travel down into the chest and all the way to the diaphragm, that help us breathe. We have a mnemonic that goes like this; "three, four and five keep the diaphragm alive". If the victim is stabbed above the third cervical level, this is invariably fatal. The victim will suffocate to death over the following few minutes as the diaphragm and all other muscles below the neck are paralysed. The particularly frightening thought is that such a victim can potentially remain conscious, able to hear and see their attacker as they gradually suffocate to death.

Armed with this level of detail, I took my information to the police. I felt the need to explain how high the knife penetrated my neck, how deep the injury was, the upward projection of the blade and what could have happened if the knife was just two centimetres to the right. My case officer politely acknowledged my expertise and my feelings. He was a true gentleman and looking back at my behaviour then, it was not something I am proud of. Eventually I conceded. I felt I had put my professional background to use, I had put my case across as best as I could, and I had to accept the fact that in the grand scheme of things this level of detail is not really critical. This was probably the most frustrating part of my entire experience. I recall my frustration getting the better of me once when I was angry on the phone to my case officer and I remember saying, "Does anyone give a toss how close I came to death?" It was at that moment that I partly came to my senses. Probably, I needed to get angry that one time in order to realise just how silly I had been.

Much later, I was offered the courtesy of meeting the head of the CPS. This was something that I greatly appreciated as I thought at last someone might be willing to listen to me. I took the opportunity to shake off these niggles and I asked the same question: "Does it matter how close to death I came?" I felt a bit uneasy asking but as I looked at his face, I got the gist of it. He smiled at me, acknowledged the question, and leaned back in his chair. It slowly dawned on me; he wanted me to understand the purpose of my question. The truth is it does matter, but not as much as I thought it should. This is how eventually I came to understand the issue. The law addresses two distinct matters, which are culpability and harm. When stabbing a victim in the neck, the potential for harm is addressed through culpability. The extent of the harm caused is then addressed in its own right. Obviously the more the harm, the harsher the sentence. How close a victim came to being killed is of importance in defining the level of culpability, but it is only one part of a bigger picture. There it was, I finally had my answer, and it came with a smile.

With that said, I do not totally regret what I did. There was, possibly, a positive outcome to my frustrating persistence. At some stage I came to realise that initially the only medical evidence the police had was the A&E statement. Unfortunately, this statement barely (please excuse the pun) scratched the surface. I personally had provided such statements in the past and I knew what such a document tended to include. It would include reference to a wound of such-and-such a width, to a scan with a conclusion that there was no deep-seated injury, that I had a few stitches and that I was sent home the same day without the need for a follow up. That is about it! Any independent observer will conclude from such a statement that this was no more than a simple cut to the skin. After all, the scan said so. I have a strong feeling though that my persistence, even though it was somewhat misguided, had the effect of readdressing to some degree the level of culpability. I presume there would be a difference in culpability between someone just trying to cut their victim with a knife as opposed to someone plunging a knife deep into their victim's neck, intending more harm, possibly wanting to kill. I honestly believe that my persistence with the scan did shift the culpability and did influence what happened later. Or at least I like to think so.

Despite the scan, the story of the knife was not complete until our case officer brought my shirt back after the trial concluded. I hadn't seen my shirt since I gave it to the officer on the first night. When I had taken it off, I hadn't look at it closely, and why would I? It came back to me in a plastic evidence bag, all crumpled up. As I shook it down, I saw the blood, which was a shock. That was the first time I realised I did in fact bleed, because on the night there was no blood on my hand. In that early video where I clutched my neck, I remember that as I took my hand off, I looked at it and there was no blood. I still thought then that someone must have hit me with a bat or an iron bar. When I examined the shirt closely, I could see the knife had torn into the shirt before it went into my neck, from below, going upwards, just as I had thought from my scan. But from my shirt, I could see that the angle was steep, almost vertical, not as the scan showed. Another thing that didn't immediately match up was that the tear in the shirt was at the top end of my back and it was on the right, not the left. In that moment, my analytical mind just went into overdrive. I thought I had gotten the full picture when I saw the scan, but far from it. My shirt told a different story. It was then that I understood exactly what had happened.

My heart was pounding again. I realised that he must have held the knife in his right hand with his arm down by his side as he snuck up behind me. He must have been perfectly in line behind me as I remember seeing nothing before the stabbing. But then, thank God, the path leading up to the hall takes a gentle turn to the right. It must have been at that moment that he started to swing at me, but by then I must have moved just a couple of centimetres to his right. He must have swung at me upwards from right to left just as one would from where his right hand was. The tip of the knife tore into my shirt just below my shoulder level on the right before it penetrated my collar on the left. As he held the knife, the blade was at an angle. I could see from the penetration in my collar that the knife was not horizontal but oblique. Effectively the width of the knife was narrowed, causing less harm. But the most incredible thing was that as the knife struck my collar it changed direction just slightly. It did not carry on in the same upward trajectory. Out of all places, the knife pierced my collar where it was thickest and doubled up. The collar itself is no more than two to three centimetres wide, and the knife hit it spot on. That must have been one of my angels that day. The thickness of the collar must have absorbed just enough force, stopping the tip of the knife just short of my major vessels. I was incredibly, incredibly fortunate. The chances of surviving such a callous swing are less that one in a hundred. If he was a couple of centimetres nearer, if he was a couple of centimetres to my right, if the path remained straight, if he held the knife slightly differently, if he stabbed me just a second earlier or a second later, and so many other if's, I would not be here today. There is a very narrow corridor in the neck where the least harm is caused, and the knife rested in that corridor. It was a large kitchen knife, about 5 cm wide at its base, and given that my wound was about 5 cm wide it was clear that the blade went in at least far enough to its widest part. But it went in obliquely, and it went into this corridor; not even a small vein in my neck was touched. It was a stab with surgical precision on a moving target by an uncontrolled swing. I just kept looking at my shirt and for a few minutes I said nothing.

That Wednesday evening, after I saw the scan, I went back home and carried on answering all the cards and letters we received. I remember receiving two cards from Altrincham Grammar School for Girls signed by all the pupils in a couple of classes. There was a card signed by all the residents on Grove Lane. Someone had taken the trouble to knock on each and every door just to wish me well. There was a card from a complete stranger in London who told me how moved he was by my forgiveness and that he had donated on my behalf to a charity close to my heart. How did he know, or was it just a coincidence? The cards just kept on coming, hundreds of them. Boxes of chocolate, flowers, fruit baskets, it was overwhelming. Our music teacher who we have known for years commented that she only saw such a response when someone sadly passed away, who would naturally never see these expressions of love by others. Despite the shock of going through my scan, by the evening I was feeling extremely happy and content.

A friend of mine had arranged for me to meet two people with legal backgrounds that evening. I knew one of them very well as he lived locally and had previously attended my study circle. The other I had met a few times at community events. We talked mainly about the charge of section 18 and the fact that there was no hate-crime element to the charge. I sensed that, like many of my friends and colleagues, they were unhappy about that and they wanted to check if I felt similarly, and if I needed legal support. They both felt it was a let-down and suggested that possibly my background and my forgiveness may have played a part. They asked me if I wanted to pursue the matter further, if I wanted to object formally, legally, whatever. I was listening to them, but by then I was in a different mood having just read so many cards. I wasn't fully concentrating on every word they said, but instinctively I was not comfortable with the proposed idea at all. There I was, sitting with two legal advocates, just what I thought I needed, but somehow complaining or challenging did not sit well with me. They were both sitting there thinking here is your chance, but it felt alien to me, and I honestly don't know why. I told them how much I appreciated them coming and offering me support at such a difficult time, but I was not sure that I wanted to challenge. I distinctly recall that as we were having this discussion late Wednesday night, my neck started aching. My neck was telling me that it was not the right thing for me to do. I instinctively knew that for me to recover quickly and fully, I needed to stay positive, and I needed to think positively, just as I had been doing so far.

Over the years I have come across many patients that have suffered horrendous injuries and yet I saw in them a strength of character, resilience and resolve. Their acceptance and the fact they complained so little must have rubbed off on me somehow. My decision was final. I was not going to challenge. Physically and emotionally, I could not afford to challenge, not when there was still a good deal of healing to go through. That night I did ask Syrsa what she thought about challenging the charge of Section 18, and she also said no. For me, that was just as good a reason as any!

As I lay in bed that night, I couldn't help thinking how lucky I was. Earlier that evening Syrsa had told me about a stabbing incident in Rochdale that had been on the news that day. The story was that of a man sitting in his car minding his own business when he was stabbed in the back of his neck. The news mentioned that the man was in a stable condition, but he had suffered a life-changing injury and Syrsa wasn't very sure what that meant. In this unfortunate young man's stabbing, the tip of the knife must have found its way into the spinal cord and I assumed he was paralysed. I was not comfortable with the way I was thinking that night. I remember feeling saddened by the news, but equally I couldn't help feeling how lucky I was to have gotten away with it so lightly. Life can be cruel, and it didn't make much sense to me other than I needed to be very thankful.

Chapter 9

Getting a Grip

Thursday brought its own unique challenges, things I had not been expecting. There had seemed to be nothing unusual about the morning and I remember on my way to hospital I was looking forward to the training day ahead. Throughout the day I was feeling an unusual buzz, as if I was 'charged up'. I don't know how to describe the feeling, but I am sure it must have been all those endorphins inside me still going full blast. It was completely different to the calm I felt on the night of the stabbing. To be frank, it was generally a pleasant feeling. I was feeling more assertive, and I was engaging and instinctive more than usual, but I also kept doing silly things. For instance, I felt so good within myself that I started thinking about the young man who stabbed me. I felt a strong need to reach out to him. It did not feel right that I should have felt so good, yet he was cooped up in custody. The difficulty I had was that I did not know what to do, who to speak to.

Eventually, and for no sane reason, I emailed Rob Smith from ITV who had interviewed me a few days earlier. It was one of these emails where as soon as you hit the send button, you think to yourself "What an idiot, you can't be serious". But that was exactly the sort of confused mood I was in and I started having difficulty controlling myself. The past four days had been intensely emotional, and I was becoming too impulsive for my own liking. I have since looked back at this email and somehow, I can see the sense of what I was doing then. My mind was racing with many thoughts and I was worried that in time I would forget about them. When I wrote to Mr Smith, I was making a commitment to my thoughts and to my feelings, and that included a commitment to Ian, as I started to use my attacker's proper name. But this buzz, this energy, just kept going and it had a significant impact on my behaviour and my decisions over the next two years. I was behaving in a way that I never imagined myself able to. I wasn't just feeling more energetic, I also felt more assertive, more determined and much less inhibited. I found myself getting involved more readily and doing things that I never would have done before. It is not that I needed much encouragement, but the way I felt was as if I could handle anything on top of my busy work schedule.

This may sound all well and good, but over time I found that the energy was unfocused, it did not have a clear purpose. I had a strong urge to do something, to be involved, but I did not know how or what this should be. In the first few months, given the opportunity, I would attend events on anything to do with hate, knife crime, victim support, discrimination, Islamophobia and so on. For example, within two weeks of the stabbing, I found myself attending a No to Hate (No2H8) function in London hosted by Faith Matters. Two amazing things happened to me that evening. The first was the fact that the taxi driver—a London taxi driver—recognised me and told me that I made his day! The second was that during the evening I was given the stage for a minute and I recall saying, "I was complacent about my own crime. I am not going to be complacent again." I don't know what made me say that, but I think I was again making a commitment to be involved.

Reflecting back on that Thursday, regrettably, something else happened, and it wasn't just me doing silly things. I realised how easily this buzz, the assertiveness, the lack of inhibition impacted my ego. With all the attention I received since the stabbing, I am sure it started to feed my ego, far too quickly for me to get a grip. Thursday evening, I had my weekly study circle. I didn't want to cancel the meeting because, ever since the stabbing, I hadn't been back to our centre. I also had another duty to fulfil, the prostration of gratitude. If you are a football fan, you may have seen Mo Salah going down on his knees and prostrating after scoring a goal, and if your memory is good, Mo Farah used to do the same whenever he won a race. This is what Muslims call the prostration of gratitude. It is thanking the Almighty, and I still needed to do mine. That evening, I drove to the centre on my own and parked in the usual place. I took my prayer mat with me and went to the spot where I was stabbed. As I walked past the same iron gate and up the path, my heart was racing a bit, but I did not feel frightened, and I did not look behind. I laid my mat on the ground and prostrated to the Almighty for what had happened to me. This simple act meant a great deal to me and it was probably one of the last steps I needed to take on my road to recovery. I then proceeded to my study circle.

Normally, I have a handful of friends attending my circle, but that evening, the library was packed. I knew they were there to support me and help me recover and it turned out to be an amazing session. However, it wasn't easy going by any stretch. I spoke about the incident and what had happened over the intervening days, but it didn't take us long before we were on the topic of forgiveness. For me, my forgiveness had been spontaneous, instinctive, it wasn't something I had thought through, pre-planned. In a sense, I had forgiven with my heart, not with my head, and when you take such a spontaneous decision, there is no escaping the fact that this reflects who you are. That evening was the first time my forgiveness was open to discussion. It was intimidating, in part as I felt it wasn't just forgiveness that was being questioned, but so too the person I was. There were some deeply uncomfortable questions, but in my study circle I have always adopted the policy than no question is off limits. This is the only way to learn. Was it right to forgive somebody attacking a Muslim on the grounds of a mosque? Would doing so risk giving license for other people to do similar or worse things in the future? These were just some of the questions that we discussed.

On the whole, the mood was very positive and most of those present were supportive of what I did. I sensed that it wasn't the act of forgiveness that was being questioned, but the fact that there was no expression of anger or condemnation in response to such a violent attack on a fellow Muslim on the grounds of his mosque. But the truth is, forgiveness meant exactly that; no anger, no condemnation, otherwise it is meaningless. But more serious for me was the insinuation that what I did could have undermined the legal process. The feeling that my attacker would have been charged with attempted murder but for the fact that I expressed my forgiveness was mentioned again. Thus, my attitude had somehow paved the way for a lesser charge. The discussion was difficult because some felt that the justice system is not even-handed when it came to Muslims and that I should wise up to this fact. By the end, I couldn't help but feel that I may have let some of my friends down, not because what I did was wrong, but because I was unable to articulate my thoughts on forgiveness well enough. At the time, all I could say was that what I did felt right, I felt right. With some of the questions it seemed as if I needed to seek approval for what I did. I remember on occasions I was becoming defensive and irritated. It was definitely a challenging session but, on the whole, I felt it was positive and something that I needed. I had to get out of my comfort zone, and I needed to face up to other points of view. What I didn't realise was how defensive and irritated I was. I did not cope well with being challenged; it was probably just too early.

I remember that by the end of the session, I made the decision that I wanted to give the Friday sermon the following day. I felt the need to assert my understanding of forgiveness and explain what it meant to me and to challenge the misconceptions that we had been discussing for the past two hours. On reflection, I think it was more akin to asserting rather than explaining. In the sermon, you can express your opinion without being challenged on the spot! But then my colleagues came to me and politely told me that I should perhaps not give the sermon the following day. I don't know why, but in the heat of that moment it became more about my ego and less about forgiveness. I was not ready to cope with such a let-down and I was totally wrong in the way I took this news. In my state of mind, I felt as though they were not interested in what I had to say. The impact of one's ego on one's perception is frightening, and in the mood I was in, I didn't see this coming. I nodded my acceptance, but I recall feeling very angry and upset.

The following morning, I had a phone call from a very close colleague from the mosque. I am sure he sensed how I felt the previous evening and probably just wanted to make sure I was fine. But as soon as he started to talk, I remember I didn't even let him finish his sentence. I just went into an outburst and said, "Don't you dare speak to me about anything that is negative." I think I then said "In my state of mind I can only accept a positive conversation. If you're going to start anything with me that's going to require any dealing with negativity, don't even dare start. I am not in the mood." I do not recall how the call ended, but I still don't know what made me behave like that. It is extremely unusual for me to get into such an outburst, but when I do, invariably it is falling into one of my ego traps. My behaviour that Friday morning was utterly deplorable. I was literally out of control.

When I arrived at work, I was already in an angry mood and, soon to find out, disinhibited. I remember that as I walked into my department, there were three or four people standing just outside the entrance doors and I noticed two of them looking at me and I felt a sense of disapproval, of being judged. I have absolutely no idea what they were really thinking, if anything, but in the state of mind I was in I was not going to let it go. I went to my office, took my coat off, and then went back to confront them. I cannot recall exactly what I said but I think it was something like, "Are you doubting what I did?" They were total strangers, and I don't think they said anything at all. I certainly shocked them, and I am sure they thought "Who the hell is this guy?"

When I went back to my office, I realised I was out of control and this was not me. I had never done that before and I just don't snap at people, not like that. My behaviour was frightening. I needed to get a grip of myself. Eventually I conceded that my ego was getting out of control. The fear didn't get to me, the anger and hate didn't get to me, but my ego did. It is incredible how insidiously one's ego creeps in, especially when you are feeling good about yourself. I honestly believe that as much as courage is not the lack of fear, humility is also not the lack of one's arrogance or ego; it is facing up to them and keeping them in check. It still upsets me greatly thinking back to this, but I need to be honest. It was part of my journey, a painful part. My frame of mind was very much unsettled, prone to flights and spontaneity, for good and bad.

By the end of the morning, I managed to calm myself down before going to the Friday sermon. That sermon was a much-needed period of reflection. I prayed with the rest of our congregation after which everyone came over to give me the customary Friday hug. The first week was coming to an end. It had been an incredible week dealing with so many challenges. I just went home and had a good weekend rest. I didn't realise how much I'd needed that. By the following Monday I think I had most things under control. But now I was back to my full clinical duties and at least my work routine was getting back to normal. In all honesty, it is my routine work that keeps me sane and level-headed, and I needed to get back to it quickly. I later remember asking one of my colleagues to take the stiches out of my neck and to take a memento picture.

So, more usual time started to pass. Then, in the lead up to the trial, one Monday in early December I received a phone call from my case officer. He told me that a remote-hearing session was going to take place that morning in court. He wasn't sure, but he thought Ian might plead guilty to the charge of Section 18. I still did not fully understand what these legal processes were all about but regardless, I did not feel good about what I was hearing. I started to get a horrible feeling that if Ian pleaded guilty that morning, then that was it. It was over; no trial, nothing. To make it worse, the case officer told me that there was no need for me to attend. I had already felt excluded from the process so far, and here we were at the potentially final stages and again I was not part of it.

As soon as I put the phone down, I got dressed and drove straight to the court. There I looked at the screens outside each courtroom listing which cases were being held where, but I could not find the one I was looking for. I asked a clerk for some help and they told me that the case I was enquiring about had already been heard, and that, for whatever reason, the judge or the CPS had decided to up the charge to attempted murder. No one had spoken to me about this and I had no idea who made the decision or why. I did find out a few months later, after the trial had finished, from the head of the CPS, that the solicitor acting on behalf of the CPS had made that decision there and then, that morning. Personally, I find it hard to believe that such a decision was made wholly spontaneously. This scenario must have been thought through earlier, but I do not know what the rationale was. Nevertheless, I was immensely pleased. The decision had a great impact on my community and on the wider Muslim community across Manchester. The charge of GBH had seemed lenient and people were taking it as if it were sweeping things under the carpet. With the new charge, many of my friends felt that justice was now being served! They were very emotional, and some were almost crying on the phone to me.

That all said, I remained pragmatic. I was pleased enough with the new charge, I thought it was perfectly reasonable, but it did not much matter to me whether the charge was attempted murder or not. I was happy because I felt I might now be relevant to the judicial process, because there would still be a trial, which was then set for 12 March, three months later. I was going to have my day in court after all, and although I didn't know what that really meant, I was looking forward to it just the same. Rightly or wrongly, I always felt that by being in court I would somehow be part of the process. We shall see!

Chapter 10

The Trial

There was little that I did by way of preparation for the trial, aside from booking some annual leave for March, and little happened between the time of the plea and the trial. I just made sure that there would be an expert called to review the CT scan. Me being me, I specifically did not plan or prepare anything for that first day, as I invariably like to go into an unknown situation with an open mind. Probably some people may like to be better focused or prepared for such an occasion than I am. It may sound odd, but I find that because I don't clutter my head in advance, I venture into such a scenario with an open mind. As a consequence, I get a sense, a better feeling, about the experience and I am less likely to be distracted or judgmental. I realise that this may make me appear naïve in some circumstances but, equally, having not set myself up to expect something in particular, this enhances my ability to understand the wider context and not be biased. I had met with the case officer before the trial, so I knew the administrative details, like where it was going to be, what time we needed to be there *etc.*, and that was enough for me.

Duly, it came around. Monday morning, 12 March 2018. It had been over five months since the stabbing and finally I felt I was going to have my day in court. Neither Syrsa nor I knew what to expect, but as part of my duties as a consultant, I have given evidence in court before, mostly at a coroner's inquest, and I did not feel that attending a crown court would be particularly daunting. As expected, the trial had already generated excitement and heightened emotions within my community and many of our friends wanted to attend with us for support and a show of solidarity. I felt we were all getting a little carried away and Syrsa decided there was no need for so many to be there. That morning, after dropping Ahmad off at school, Syrsa and I started getting ready. The truth was, Syrsa was getting both of us ready! Even though it was an important occasion, the fact that it was just the two of us, it somehow felt like the good old days when we were newly married. Just the two of us on another escapade. We felt excited and anxious, but together; it felt good. We even held hands! We had planned how we were going to get to Minshull Crown Court the previous night, and there is a car park next to the court, so it should be a doddle. We set off thinking we had left enough time to get there, but there were roadworks and we ended up arriving 10-15 minutes late. By then we were more anxious than excited and, silly as it may sound, the thought occurred to me that they may not let us in! I had waited five months and now I may have messed it up.

As we rushed into the building my case officer was patiently waiting for us and reassured me that we would be going in, but we needed to wait a little while as proceedings had already started. I took some time to get a feel of the courthouse. There was a large foyer, a security entrance, TV screens next to each courtroom, bright glossy floors and serious-looking people walking around, mostly dressed in black. It was a cold and not very welcoming environment, but I suppose it was never intended to be otherwise. I did eventually find out where the canteen and the prayer room were. My case officer started to explain what was going on. The trial had not actually started; we were still in the pretrial preamble. It was not vital for us to go in if we didn't want to. I understood that in the preamble the defence presents some arguments, the prosecution likewise, and between them and the judge they set the scene for how the trial is to run. I presumed this would include what is admissible, what is not admissible, those kinds of legal things, before the jury is sworn in. I thought to myself this is not something I was going to miss. I felt the need to witness the whole experience. I remember that my case officer went into the courtroom a couple of times and eventually said we could go in now, but we needed to be quiet and to switch our phones off. We first went through the outer doors into a dark and short access-corridor and then the courtroom doors opened. At that moment, the first impact I felt was as if I had just gone back in time.

It was a large hall, no windows, strikingly dark and the voices of those speaking were distant. I could see the judge from a distance. His position was elevated; you couldn't miss him. He was a petite man, sitting up there in his ceremonial costume. As I walked in, the hall was laid out with rows of benches in the centre facing the judge. I saw the two barristers positioned along the same row but quite far apart, with probably five or six metres between them. I later realised that the barrister nearer to us as we walked in was for the prosecution, a petite young lady who had a smile on her face and who kept moving. At the far end was the barrister for the defence. He struck me as very economical with his movements, giving the impression he was relaxed, with not a single movement on his face, or indeed on much of his body, that was unnecessary. He appeared older than the prosecution barrister and came across as an intriguing person. It was those two that first caught my eye as they were stood up. Further right, there was a seating area at right angles to the central benches which I assumed would be for the jury later on. To my left-hand side, there was another seating area for the public, but this one faced forward, towards the judge. It was separated from the main hall by tall glass panels that I could see through, but which dampened the voices of the barristers. I eventually sat nearer the aisle next to a gap between the glass panels to make sure I heard as much as I could. The entrance to this seating area was at the front which meant we had to walk past those who had already arrived earlier with inevitable eye-to-eye contact. Immediately in front of that, and slightly elevated, was the witness box, which faced directly towards the jury. As I walked towards the front, I did not notice what was behind me. It was only when I turned into the seating area that I saw Ian for the first time. I couldn't stop to look at him as it would have been too obvious, but in that second or so I saw a young man behind a big glass window at the back end of the court room, dressed in grey, sat, handcuffed, with three officers flanking him. With the courtroom being dark, the view into that glass window was unmissable. It was a little bit more than a glance, but I did not have the chance to look him in the eye. Even in such a short time though, there was a lot that I could see. What struck me most was the fact he was handcuffed. We were probably six or eight metres from each other, it was all too quick, and I needed to keep walking towards my seat.

As I walked up the seating area, the ceiling-high glass panels obscured the view so I couldn't see him anymore, but then I saw sitting in the front rows what I assumed was his family. First row was mum, and second row was a young man and a young woman sitting together. I later understood that the young man was Ian's brother, and he was with his partner. I then realised why his mum was sitting in the front row. She was just ahead of the glass panels. As she leaned forward and turned her head sharply, she could just about see her son. It was practically impossible to see him sitting anywhere else. The third row was still empty, so me and my case officer sat there, just behind Ian's brother. I Instinctively wanted to sit close to them. As I passed the second row, I did exchange eye contact with the brother. I don't recall how I felt, but I remember spotting something on the brother's face, a teardrop tattoo, I think it was under his right eye. I have seen this tattoo before in a film. I am not a film buff, but there are images that tend to stick in your mind and strangely enough this was one of them. I had definitely seen that tattoo in one of Eddie Murphy's films (in my younger days) and, for whatever reason, I remembered what it meant, or at least what I thought it meant. I whispered to my case officer, "Did you see the tattoo? I think it means he is probably in a gang or he must have done something serious." I don't know what compelled me to open my mouth, but I soon realised how easy it is for a mind to be so prejudiced. I thought I spoke discreetly to my case officer, but the brother heard me, and he turned around and politely said, "That's because I lost my little kid." In that moment I wished the ground would open up and swallow me. I felt like an absolute p****. I later found out that such a tattoo also represented sorrow and loss. What an opening to the trial. If ever I thought I was on a higher moral ground, I just fell straight through it. I was ashamed of myself. Just because he was associated with Ian and just because he had a tattoo that I thought meant something, my mind immediately made a judgement, a very horrible one.

With that said, I think my horrendous remark was just the icebreaker we both needed. The two of us definitely made a connection! I later apologised to the brother for my ignorance, and he seemed to be okay with it. Yes, in that moment, he turned out to be the better man. I think that blow to my ego was just what I needed that morning. I never forgot it, and in all honesty, I was not going to let myself do so.

114 A REPLY TO HATE

Another lesson in humility which I probably needed to help me cope with the rest of the trial. I was much calmer after that.

I sat there listening carefully to what the two barristers were saying. Being late, I had already missed some of the preamble, but I tried to make sense of what I was hearing. It wasn't easy to follow, but it gradually started to make some sense. The defence barrister appeared to be highlighting the issue of mental health. I thought I heard him say that Ian had been struggling with his mental health in prison and that his medication had been increased. I vaguely picked up the name of the medication and when I went home later that evening, I looked it up and then spoke to a psychiatry colleague to get a better understanding. I quickly realised mental health was not my strong point and I left it at that. However, being from a clinical background, I do tend to pick up on little things, things that are critical in my profession, but probably not so in a legal setting. For instance, the reference to the medication dose was not accurate, but I assumed this was not important. If the same inaccuracy happened in a clinical setting, that would be deemed as an incident needing investigation. It was not easy sitting there, listening and not being overanalytical. Not easy to shake off who you are, perhaps.

I then listened to the defence barrister discussing some bodycam footage. This was the first time I learned of this footage. I got the sense that he was aiming to have this evidence excluded from the trial. I am not sure, but in response to that, I think the judge proposed what seemed to be a compromise. They would go through the bodycam evidence before deciding if it would be deemed admissible. That proved to be a fantastic idea. In effect, this meant I was going to have the chance to see the entire footage before the trial started. This may sound silly, but having the opportunity to see the footage meant I could now put missing pieces of my puzzle in place. It also meant that even if it was deemed inadmissible, at least I would have the chance to see it. Up till that point, I knew very little. In fact, odd as it may sound, I did not even have a clue how little I knew. Anyway, the bodycam evidence was ultimately permitted to be used in evidence, which also meant I had the chance to see the footage again. That was more than I could have asked for and that made me very happy. Well, not immediately so.

When the decision was made to view the footage, we all sat there waiting. The disc was with the prosecution barrister. She played it on her laptop, and it worked. They tried it on the court room's AV system, and it didn't work. This seemed unbelievable in a crown court. I was laughing within myself. Over the years, I have come across so many embarrassing encounters with an AV system refusing to respect the occasion. Meetings, conferences, seminars, junior doctors, professors, I have seen it all, but not in a courtroom. Somehow, audio-visual systems have no respect whatsoever for any profession. As ever, everyone appeared to remain calm. I don't have full recollection of all that went on, but I remember that eventually everyone started to see the funny side. Everyone tried hard to make it work, but technology was not shifting for anybody. I think even a new monitor was brought in at some stage. For a brief moment, we started to see a picture, but there was no sound. With all that was going on, I felt the judge remained very calm and did not appear to be phased or irritated. It was nice to see that even a judge had to surrender to such ill fortune, probably he has also seen it all before. That Monday, the AV system was not going to budge, and the decision was eventually made to pack it up and resume the following day.

With all that was going on, I felt that the atmosphere in that courtroom became more humane; the air of formality softened a bit. I thought about Ian behind the glass window and I was saddened. As he sat there, he had no influence whatsoever on the people who were about to decide his fate. Through his actions, he ended up giving away so much agency. That is how the court felt that day; it was about deciding the fate of this person and all he could do was watch and listen. He had no part to play whatsoever. Unless you actually see that person sat there, cuffed, totally unable to make a difference to their own life, it may be difficult to empathise. Everyone present that day was there because of his violent crime, and yet, somehow, I couldn't help but feel sorry for him. I was struggling somewhat with my feelings but when I spoke to Syrsa about it she reminded me how difficult this would have been for his own family, especially his mum. Having gone through the day's experience, we were no longer feeling as excited as we were earlier on.

The following day and from then onwards, I made sure we arrived on time, so we ditched the car and used the tram instead. The AV equipment was as obstinate as ever. Eventually, everyone admitted defeat and we moved to another courtroom in the afternoon. This was to be the first time I saw the bodycam footage, which became very important for me; it was the missing part of my story that I knew nothing about, and no one was going to share it with me except in a court of law. I cannot stress how vital this can be for a victim.

We all sat together, watching the footage for the first time. I saw five, probably six officers arriving at this young man's house. They knock on the door, he answers quite casually, a few words were exchanged and soon afterwards he was being arrested. It looked surreal. Ian didn't seem phased at all. I was listening carefully to the recording and I think I heard him say, "I wanted to kill somebody", and then it was something like "It was either killing my brother or killing someone else", and "I had to kill somebody", "Have I killed him?", "Is he dead?" He mentioned the desire to kill probably more than 15 times. The police were impressively calm, but I also got the sense that they were being meticulous. If I'm not mistaken, I think the officer in charge said something like "You'd better do it right—I don't want them to rip me another back passage." I guessed she must have been in court recently and evidence she oversaw had been discredited. She was making sure this time everyone was doing their jobs professionally. It was very busy footage and sometimes difficult to follow, and I later came to realise that the prosecution's entire case would rest on what Ian had said during this arrest. His own words were going to be used in evidence against him. In total contrast to how much he was saying on this footage, I later understood that once he was in custody, he kept his mouth shut. The footage was the only damning evidence. On this footage, he was also heard saying "I don't care if I go to prison for all my life." He spoke of his frustration about his mental health and I think more than once he said, "I'm going crazy."

As I watched the footage, I could not help but feel that the police were brilliant in what they did. I am sure in the back of the sergeant's mind, she must have already figured that what Ian was saying needed to be admissible, and therefore they needed to be very careful. After all, this is exactly what the defence barrister was doing just now, five months on. I don't think at any point Ian was asked a leading question that could be construed as formal interrogation. The officers just let him speak freely while being filmed. I am not entirely sure when he was formally arrested, as he was then read his rights including the classic line "You have the right to remain silent. Anything you say can be used against you in court...". Despite that, Ian just carried on talking while everyone waited for the prisoner transport vehicle. This is now my guesswork, but I think as Ian's brother was arrested just a short time earlier, the transport vehicle was already in use, and this allowed the officers to carry on talking to Ian while they waited. In any case, waiting for that vehicle allowed Ian to keep talking; sitting with officers in a police van who just chatted with him. This is what the defence barrister was unhappy about and wanted excluded. The judge decided there was nothing untoward and that the footage could be included. All I could think then was well done to the police for a fantastic job. The prosecution barrister looked as though she had just won the preliminary battle, and so she should. But I was surprised that the gleam in her eyes was not matched by any expression of disappointment on the defence barrister's face. He looked utterly unperturbed.

As we watched the footage, I noticed something that looked very odd and made me worried. The clock on the bodycam was an hour out. I was stabbed shortly after 17:30, and Ian was arrested about an hour later. But the bodycam clock said he was being arrested at 17:30, just before he committed his crime! I quickly guessed the bodycams must have been on GMT still. When I saw that, my first instinct was to keep my mouth shut. It seemed that nobody had spotted this, as nobody made any mention of it, and after all, I was probably the only one who recalled exactly when I was stabbed. I had a very uncomfortable feeling in my stomach. What would happen if they actually spot this? Will this evidence be thrown out of court? I think I probably overreacted as the next day I did confess to my case officer that I'd noticed it, but he didn't seem perturbed.

During his arrest, it struck me that Ian had realised his brother had been arrested, and he was saying, "It's not him. It's me." Then towards the end of the footage I am sure I heard him say, "You'll see me on the CCTV camera outside the mosque." I don't think anyone had picked up on that either. They may have heard it and probably thought a mosque is a mosque. But our mosque is a church. Unless you are local, no one knows that this mosque is a repurposed church. Ian did not live locally. So, how did he know that this was a mosque, and how did he know that there was CCTV outside it? For him to get to the mosque from where his brother's house is, he would have needed to take at least four purposeful turns to end up on Grove Lane. I felt at the time that at the least this should have been looked into, even if nothing conclusive was proved. I thought I deserved as much. Was it just a coincidence? I will never know, and probably by that stage it did not matter anymore.

That was the gist of the bodycam footage and Tuesday was coming to an end. The prosecution was able to use this evidence, and as the trial unfolded, it transpired that to all intents and purposes, that this was to be the main bulk of the evidence. As an ordinary member of the public and having watched the footage I would have to endorse that approach. I thought "This guy has nailed himself." How many times do you need to hear someone say "I want to kill" before you decide that this was what he meant to do? It was a no-brainer. I honestly thought the defence barrister was going to be gutted when the judge passed his decision.

That Tuesday, and as we moved to another court room, I took the opportunity to sit next to Ian's mother. I wanted to break the ice with her, to have her feel at ease rather than intimidated by my presence. I introduced myself and we spoke a little, not much, but more than just simple introductions. I cannot recall what we spoke about, but my intention was simply to break the ice and I am happy to say that we did.

Wednesday morning, we went back to court and we saw how the jury were sworn in. Having witnessed the process first-hand with Syrsa, we were simply amazed at the fairness of it all. Since then, whenever the situation arose, we tell people when it comes to selecting a jury, if you are going to get a fair trial, you will get it here. We initially saw 15 jurors ushered in. Out of the 15 a lot was drawn and 12 were selected at random. When they were sworn in, I could hear two of them were sworn using the Quran, four used the Bible and six used the affirmation. They were a mix of ages and they were black, white and Asian. I think there were seven women and five men. There was no bias, just a group of average, ordinary people. They were going to listen to the evidence and then make a judgement. There was no preponderance of one sex, one age group, one religious or racial background over another. It looked to me and to Syrsa very fair. Another thing we noticed that morning was that for three consecutive days, Ian's father was not there. Only his mum, and she was there every day. Later on, I realised that Ian's father was ill, and that his mum works and also looks after her father who was not well. I couldn't help but think that this must have been a very difficult week for her.

At last, the jury was sworn in that morning and the trial started in the afternoon. I listened to the opening statement from my prosecution barrister, and she opened by saying to the jury, "This is not a religiously motivated crime." That was her opening statement! My jaw dropped and I just thought to myself, "Keep your bloody mouth shut". That same opening statement was later used as the headline in the newspapers. Ian had never said anything about what motivated him to stab me. In fact, it was my understanding that the motive for the stabbing was not investigated beyond what was witnessed on the bodycam footage. Both Syrsa and I had already had this argument between us and came to the conclusion that there was no strong evidence to conclusively support either view, so we left it at that. The fact that such an emphatic statement was used as the opening remark stunned me. That was the moment that I felt the judicial system was unfair, and it did not make sense to me. However, I thought who am I to question her professionalism? The prosecution barrister must have had her reasons, probably her instructions to say this, but I didn't see that one coming.

The case for the prosecution carried on and I sat listening about me being a victim who was simply the wrong person in the wrong place at the wrong time, that kind of thing. Then, I listened to her describing the extent of my injury. She simply read out the report by a radiologist describing what I previously saw on the scan. I understood every word that she was saying, but I immediately realised that no one else in that courtroom had any idea what she was talking about. That day, the only person in that courtroom who knew precisely where the knife blade came to rest was me. I was the only one who knew I was no more than two centimetres from being killed. Sadly, the prosecution couldn't even pronounce some of the structures in the report correctly. One word that neither the barrister nor the judge pronounced correctly was 'carotid'. Then I recalled a colleague's suggestion had been to take a 3D model to let the jury see where the knife was. I realised then that probably he was not being dramatic after all; he was being practical. How can a jury understand technical jargon and what it meant? They were not told at what level I was stabbed. They were not shown a picture of the wound on my neck. If my registrar had described the injury and the scan to me in the same manner, he would have been rollicked. As a senior consultant sitting there, I didn't know whether to laugh or cry. That session looked a bit amateurish to me. They were not shown the shirt where the knife sliced cleanly through my collar, but most frustratingly, the knife itself was not even brought to court. The jury were only shown a picture of the knife taken at a distance.

At the time, I was not openly questioning the process, as it was not for me to do so. I simply sat and listened and tried to understand. I kept checking myself that I could be wrong in how I was interpreting what was unfolding in front of me. But when I spoke to people afterwards, many were equally baffled by what had taken place. As the victim and a witness to my crime, I was not asked to give evidence. The whole process felt as if I had absolutely nothing to do with it. I was listening to my case as if I did not exist. But then it dawned on me; this is not about me, it never was. It is about the defendant. It was during the trial that I started to realise what 'the criminal justice system' meant. It is justice for the defendant, and rightly so. Once I got that into my head, I started to feel a bit more settled and a bit less critical.

I shouldn't take it personally, so to speak. Witnessing my trial was a great experience for me and a great eyeopener. It gave me an understanding of the legal system that I would never have had otherwise. What I came to understand is that the criminal justice system, the court, the trial, none are about the victim; all are concerned with the defendant. Justice for the victim can only be served when the police do their job properly, when the evidence is sound and when the prosecution is well prepared. I can now sympathise when I hear about victims struggling with the judicial process, about victims feeling that they have not received justice. The hard truth from a victim's point of view is that a court's primary function is to secure justice for the defendant. Everything in the courtroom has been designed to be as fair as possible to the defendant, and that is how it should be.

Later that Wednesday and as everyone was getting ready to go home, I was told that all hell was breaking loose outside the court building. I rushed to see what was going on and I saw Ian's brother very angry, shouting and gesticulating at people, and then I spotted the ITV film crew. He was shouting, "They wanted us to look like racists. We are not racist." I thought he was on the verge of assaulting the crew. I am not sure, but I think they may have asked him a question about the motive, and he just went ballistic. I went up to him and I grabbed him. In fact, not really grabbed him, but embraced him and started to calm him down. It was a firm embrace and I was not going to let go until he calmed down. I did not want him to say or do anything that would get him into trouble. He really looked angry and shaken and kept on swearing. I had to grab him firmly, but he knew who I was, and he didn't fight me off. It took a couple of minutes, but he started to calm down. I literally stood there as a barrier between him and the film crew and slowly moved him away. I then told him, "I'm not going to let them do that. You have my word. You have to trust me." I kept on repeating my words to reassure him that no matter what, I will not let this happen. He finally believed me, and I let go. That was the second time I connected with Ian's brother and I felt I may have redeemed myself. He then simply walked away.

There I was, on the one hand struggling with how the prosecution opened her case while on the other hand it appeared as if the media was trying to stir up the 'hate' angle, or at least this was what Ian's brother perceived, and I was there defending him. It felt very strange, but this was again another eyeopener for me. Through Ian's brother, I had a glimpse of how it can make you feel to be branded a racist. To be accused of something that you are not. I realised that should I decide to pursue the angle of hate, it was not just about me and Ian. Even if I didn't try, I would be implicating his family, his friends and his community with nothing more than guilt by association. Facts in this regard are not the be all end all; it is about perceptions and prejudices. So much harm can be done before we are anywhere near seeing the truth.

What I saw through the brother's anger was a lesson to hate peddlers. It inflames a raging fire that has no interest in who it burns. That encounter had a profound impact on me. I am so happy that I was there, that I saw his anger and felt it. From then on, I became very careful in how I answered the question of why I think he stabbed me. All this stayed with me and I later changed my press-release statement because of this encounter. In the statement that I would give following the verdict I said, "No one is responsible for Ian's crime except Ian", and I refused to answer the question of "Why do I think he stabbed me?" I remember going home that Wednesday evening absolutely shattered. It had been very emotional but there was still more to come.

Thursday morning, I saw the defence barrister speaking to the judge. Ian was going to take the witness stand. The barrister did not want the jury to see Ian walking to the stand, handcuffed and escorted by police officers. It was argued that such a vision could be prejudicial. He requested that before the jury was allowed in, Ian should already be seated in the witness box, cuffed at the ankles, and not shadowed by police. That started me thinking. That barrister knows very well what impacts a jury's perceptions and how little things can sway the balance of their judgement. He was not even going to allow the jury to see the handcuffs, and then I recalled how I felt when I first saw them. That made me all the more frustrated. I felt the defence barrister was on a different level altogether. But then I wondered, surely all these tactics are not going to get your client out of the hole he has already dug for himself. Everyone heard what was recorded on the bodycams; he did not have a chance.

We all waited a little while until Ian was safely seated at the witness box and then we were allowed in. As I entered and sat down, Ian turned towards me and said, "Dr Kurdy, I'm sorry." I really was not expecting that. It just came out of the blue and in that moment, I did not know what to feel. I was not prepared for his apology. I later felt sad about how I reacted in that moment. Was that apology really for me? I should have taken it at face value. I don't recall if the jury were already in, but I recall wondering whether he said that from his heart or if he was told to say it. Three days in court and having listened to the prosecution barrister the day before, I was now the worse for it. That is not me!

Anyhow, in my silly state of mind I lost my first opportunity to connect with Ian. I should have gestured to him something in return, but probably all I did was nod. Looking back at this moment, I still credit him for looking at me, straight at me, and saying "I'm sorry." By now, the jury were on their way in, and everyone was seated, poised and ready for the real show. Then the barrister for the prosecution had her moment. She was going to nail this guy. After all, she had the irrefutable evidence to convict him. By now, the jury had already seen the bodycam footage and she went straight for the jugulars. It was all about him saying "I wanted to kill." She went on and on about what he said, what he "intended" to do. After all, it was said more than 15 times in the footage.

I thought she did brilliantly well. I would not have wanted to be in that witness box facing this fierce fiery lady. There was a sense of excitement and for a while it felt as if I was watching an episode of *Kavanagh Q.C.* I allowed myself to enjoy that moment. By the time she was finished with Ian, I thought, "The poor guy, he's had it." From time to time, I looked at the defence barrister thinking any time now he will be putting his head in his hands and throwing in the towel. I had thought the prosecution had absolutely crucified Ian, but what was the defence barrister doing throughout? He was on his laptop. I was stunned! Cool as a cucumber. No reaction whatsoever, nothing. From that morning, this is the most memorable vision I still have in my mind. It was as if all that was said mattered so little, and somehow, so it transpired.

Once the prosecution finished, the defence barrister calmly stood up and turned towards the jury. He first faced them and then he started speaking. It was then that I realised, all he had to do was to instil doubt. And suddenly all the recorded talk of wanting to kill became irrelevant. It was now about whether he really meant what he said: "Did he really, really mean what he said?" All the barrister needed in order to discredit the prosecution's case was to instil doubt, no matter how slight this doubt might be. That was the name of the game. It is either about discrediting the evidence or throwing doubt at it. He looked at the jury and all he did was give them possible, plausible reasons for hearing what they had heard. Obviously, this did not include a desire to kill. One of the possibilities was that Ian simply did not care anymore. After all, he said he wanted to go to jail. He had suffered mental-health problems. Now that he was in custody, he was receiving better health care! He presented evidence that Ian was now on seven times his medication dose. Another plausible reason was that Ian wanted to protect his brother. He wanted to make sure that the police did not blame his brother for something that he had done. He then told a story along the lines of a child walking onto a frozen lake, and that child is your son or daughter. He asked the jury, to this effect, would you let your child go on that frozen lake unless you were 100 percent sure that the ice was unbreakable? At this point the judge rebuked him for the parable, and the barrister duly apologised. But the clever man had done his work.

As I listened, I was very impressed and equally astounded. Is that all that the defence needs to do? And the painful truth is, yes. It is his duty to throw doubt. As we left for our lunch break, I asked Syrsa what she thought. She said, "He's guilty." I said, "I don't think so." I thought that if I was on the jury, I would not convict because I now have my doubt. This was when I realised just how weak the case for the prosecution was. The prosecution didn't put me on the stand, she didn't ask me if I ran or if I feared for my life, she didn't ask me about the look on Ian's face. All that would probably have been unfair. But what about the hard evidence, the scan, the knife, the shirt? In fact, I was shocked when I was told that the forensic expert for the prosecution concluded that only "mild" force was used in my attack. I thought "What the flaming heck!" I was thrust forwards by the stabbing. The knife went through the collar of my shirt, it went as far as its widest point, but in forensic terms, it was concluded that this was "mild". How can that be? Ironically, the prosecution ended up accepting the defence expert's judgement in that "moderate" force was used! I knew then that no one had actually examined the knife or my shirt. I did challenge the prosecution barrister afterwards about this, and I asked if the knife was examined by a forensics expert. I sensed that no examination was made, and I am confident that the term "mild" was based on the A&E report. After all, I would have reached the same conclusion given the same information. But with that said, did the force of the stabbing have any bearing on the critical question of whether this person intended to kill? Again, probably not. Still, I would have thought that justice to the victim would have demanded at least presenting my shirt with the knife sticking through the slit to show the jury where the knife was. If not, then at least having the actual knife presented as evidence, and if not that then at least I could have been asked to expose my neck and show the scar and the indent through the skin. Did any of that matter at all? Probably not. I felt I was totally invisible to the jury, as if I did not exist. When I gave a statement to the press on Friday after the verdict, I said "The victim is irrelevant to the judicial process."

As the trial proceeded, it was interesting that the jury wanted to see the video evidence over and over again. Specifically, from the CCTV that overlooked the mosque. This video was not clear. The camera was mounted on a long pole, possibly five-six meters high. The pole was located on the other side of the road overlooking the entrance to the mosque, probably 15-20 meters from where I was stabbed. As it happens, there is a large bush on the right-hand side of the entrance which obscured the precise moment of the stabbing. In essence, there is no visual evidence of the stabbing itself at all. Unfortunately, on the day of the stabbing, the centre's own CCTV cameras failed to record. Still today no one knows why, but the CCTV cameras were recording the day before and the day after, but not when I was attacked. The bottom line is that the jury could not see Ian clearly at the moment of the stabbing. In some sense, I thought that this was a blessing for me. I don't know how I would have felt if I saw someone stabbing me. From the footage, the jury saw Ian follow me into the centre and then a few seconds later as he appeared beyond the bush chasing me, and then turning back and running away. The chase seemed to be critical to them and they requested to be shown that footage a number of times, even to the point where a screen was placed in front of them to allow them a closer look. Having witnessed that, I couldn't help but think how important it was for the jury to get a feel of what he wanted to do.

That Thursday a solicitor friend of mine attended court alongside me. I gave him my press release to read, and he took one look at it and told me it was rubbish. He said it was far too long, too wordy. I cut it down from the two pages to half a page and spent Thursday evening trying to be realistic and at the same time positive. We went in Friday morning, but the jury were still deliberating. At 14:00 they came back and declared they couldn't reach a unanimous verdict. The judge asked them if they were able to reach a 10:2 verdict and they said yes, they had reached a 10:2 verdict. The 10:2 verdict was then read out loud. The jury could not find enough evidence to convict Ian of attempted murder. The judge proceeded to thank the jury for their effort and duly acquitted Ian of that charge. However, he still needed to be sentenced as he had already pleaded guilty to Section 18. I saw his mum was happy. As she stood up, I went over to her and I told her I was happy for her, which I was, and I gave her a hug. I hadn't realised that there were reporters sitting close by watching, but it was immensely pleasing for me that this moment was mentioned by the newspapers. In my presentation on forgiveness, I show the headline from the *Daily Mirror* where they wrote "Hero surgeon who treated Manchester bomb victims, hugs mum of man who stabbed him in 'hate crime'. Dr Nasser Kurdy said he forgives the attacker Ian Rooke adding: 'Fairness and compassion underpin British values.'" I felt this was very comforting as inevitably when someone sees something good, it can be difficult to ignore. That Friday, Ahmad and Oaiss came with us to court. As they passed Ian's mum, she looked at them and said, "You are very lucky to have him as your dad."

Following the trial, I told people that I learned a great deal from the court proceedings. Yes, it was frustrating at times, but equally there were many good things. Ian's family, the judge, the jury selection, the barristers, the AV system respecting no one, the two-hour lunch breaks, the bodycam footage, the prosecution going for the throat only for the defence to duck and weave. In that week, the emotions that ran through me were immense. I am ever so grateful that I had the chance to experience all of it, especially seeing Ian and hugging his brother and then his mum. I knew from the outset that I was not there to judge or demand a guilty verdict. I was there to witness a process that was only partly about me. I may have wanted it to be all about me, but that is simply not how to administer justice.

I don't remember exactly when, but after the verdict, the defence barrister came up to me, shook my hand and said that my forgiveness has had a deep impact on Ian. He wanted to share this with me and that he himself was moved by what I did. To be honest, I was not expecting that at all, but I felt very pleased. Through forgiveness, I have always appreciated Ian as a human being, nothing less, nothing more, and to be told that this had an impact on him made me very happy. Deep inside, it was something that I wanted to know, and to be told this just after the verdict softened the impact.

Then, just before we left, the prosecution barrister gave us a few minutes to sit with her. Understandably, for her as a professional, the verdict was a disappointment. She set out to convict but failed to do so. It was then that I told her that if I was on that jury, I would most likely have acquitted Ian myself. Syrsa was still insisting she would have convicted him! But it was then that I asked her about Ian mentioning the CCTV at the mosque. She looked at me inquisitively, and I told her that our mosque isn't actually a mosque, it is a church. Grove Lane is simply a residential road. People from outside the area do not know that this is a mosque, and Ian was not local. I was not expecting a response, but she then raised her eyebrows and said sorry, she was not aware of that. Anyway, we had the chance to chat for ten minutes, which allowed for my emotions to calm down. My heart was not pounding any more, and the shaking of my hands and the tremble in my voice stopped. I had a feeling that the press would be waiting outside for me and I needed to get a hold of myself. By the time I went outside, I had the smile back on my face, and ITV was waiting for me. I really feel even now, over two years since the verdict, when I see that interview again, I am somewhat proud of myself. That interview was an honest expression of me. In those ten minutes spent with the prosecution barrister I managed to completely get rid of any feelings of negativity. I was able to deliver a short positive message with a smile and I kept my promise to Ian's brother. Again, I don't know how the hell I managed to do it, but it made me feel very happy, something that I needed for the coming few days.

As soon as we got home, everyone was on my back again. There was a rekindled sense of anger and let-down. Everyone was expecting, or hoping, for a guilty verdict. They simply could not understand what had happened. Again, I was having to cope with the frustration of so many who had a great deal of love and affection towards me. I could sense what they wanted for me, but I also knew that they were not there. They did not witness the trial; I did. As a result, that weekend I wrote a series of statements trying my best to present what I had witnessed, and to explain why the verdict was actually the correct one.

I did initially express some anger in what I wrote, but over the following days I manged to tease the anger out of my words. I was able to reassure everyone that the trial was fair. I explained what I came to understand, that the trial had to be fair to the accused and to be able to convict, there should be no doubt. In fact, my last statement was exactly about that and about the principle of doubt as understood in Islam.

In Islam, it is forbidden to judge if there is doubt and that is what the court did on that day. Both Syrsa and I felt that the principles adopted during the trial were Islamic, and we had no doubt about that. I did, however, finish my statement with a little bit of doubt myself. In a court of law, we all come across the cherished statement "I swear to tell the truth, the whole truth, and nothing but the truth." Well, when it came to telling my side of the story, perhaps the whole truth was left a little wanting.

With all that said, I want to briefly return to the Tuesday just after I was stabbed. It was then that Ian was charged with Section 18, to which he eventually pleaded guilty. But that got me thinking again. There had been an outcry at the time that the charge of Section 18 was a lesser charge. After the verdict, I discussed this with Syrsa. What would have happened if Ian had been initially charged with attempted murder? What chances did the CPS have to convict him? Surely, they must have foreseen the possibility of an acquittal. In fact, it is much more difficult to convict on a charge of attempted murder since you have to prove intent beyond any doubt. At the time of charging, the police had no idea as to the exact nature of my injury, how close I came to being killed, *etc*. In both mine and Syrsa's minds, we have absolutely no doubt that the charge of Section 18 was in fact the right charge. At the time, we were all engulfed with a deluge of emotions and we just could not see, or possibly refused to see, the sense of it all. How could we? Now that we can see the sense of it all, I feel the need to share this with everyone. I think if the CBC are still sceptical about the charge, I can tell them exactly where they can go, in a nice way that is. But then came the new charge. Once Ian pleaded guilty to Section 18, the CPS had it in the bag. They now felt confident to up the charge to attempted murder. This again was the right thing to do. I never found out who made that decision. I would want to thank them personally from the bottom of my heart. The fact that I had the opportunity to witness the trial was incredible for me. That week was immense, probably coming a close second to my first week after the stabbing. To me the verdict was never the reason I went there, it was everything else.

Sadly, there is still a twist in the tale. There was still the sentencing. I was told that at the sentencing session, I could stand up and deliver my victim impact statement. It was then that I would finally have my say in court. Finally, I could face Ian, his family, the judge and the barristers, and show them that I actually exist, that I mattered. Well, so much for what I thought. The first date for the sentencing was sometime in May, right in the middle of Ramadan. Nevertheless, I got myself mentally ready for it and took the day off, cancelling all my appointments. As you might have guessed, the session was cancelled at the last minute. The next date was suggested, thankfully this time after Ramadan. I again got myself ready, but this time I was wise enough not to cancel anything until the last minute. The session was cancelled again. Another date was set for the sentencing, but now it was towards the end of August. That was the final blow. Oaiss was starting a year at Toronto University and we had already booked the last two weeks in August to travel there and make sure he got settled. This would be the first time he was away from home by himself, and there was still so much to do. I felt gutted. My chance had been taken away from me. Again, it felt as if I did not matter. I asked if the hearing could be rescheduled on either side of our trip, but sadly, my reason was not good enough. As my luck would have it, this time the sentencing was not postponed. Ian was sentenced while I was in Toronto, and my victim impact statement was read in court on my behalf. My chance to look Ian in the eye and tell him that I was there for him was lost and, to date, I have not been able to get this chance back. That was by far the biggest let down for me, and that is where it ended. At least for a while.

Chapter 11

I4GiveH8

The following discussion looks back at the events described in the preceding chapters, it reflects on present circumstances and projects, and looks forward to future possibilities. It retains the interview-style format in which it was originally compiled as a way of preserving and presenting something of the book's broader compositional processes. The format also allowed us to explore questions which the earlier chapters raise in a way that we feel best reflects the open-ended, open-minded ways in which we have both tried to approach these questions.

DT: I want to start with a broad question, one which might at first seem obvious and which calls back to some of the things the book has already discussed, but that perhaps also allows a new angle to be brought to bear. How do you think forgiveness has changed your own life, your own outlook on life?

NK: I think in answering this question I need to explore something that is not obvious: the change that did not take place. Sometimes what we fail to see is the fact that there was no change, at all! By that I mean my life could have gone in a certain direction following such a horrific attack: I could perhaps have become someone who is withdrawn and depressed; I could have become angry; I could have become scared or terrified, or at best dysfunctional. There are many things that can happen as a result of being a victim of violence. In fact, a lot of the time when people have asked me to talk about my experience, they wanted to hear about this aspect of being a victim, and how this had affected me negatively: my fears, my anger, my anxiety. But I have never gone down that road. Of course, I wholeheartedly empathise with why someone would continue to struggle following such a violent attack. When you are the victim of violence it can really shock you to the core. You just don't seem to have the power or the will to fight it and you can easily resign yourself to being a victim. It is not unusual or unnatural to feel like that, especially early on after the violence. Depression, anxiety, why me! All these are perfectly normal feelings.

However, I honestly believe that because of my forgiving of the person who attacked me, the greatest impact on me was that I never experienced these feelings. That predictable change did not materialise. The one change that did happen, in a way, is that I steered back on track. I think of it like a car travelling in a straight line being hit and pushed off track. The immediate change is to steer it back straight again. For me, the strength in forgiveness is that it is more powerful than the original insult.

So, I never experienced those predictable changes. To me and to my family that was a huge positive, but somehow there is no outward expression of the positive aspect of someone just being normal. People who don't know me and don't know otherwise just see me going back to work, going back to doing my normal things, with nothing amiss. I honestly think that this was the most incredible thing that happened to me. Only those who have had an experience similar to mine could see the difference, because they have their own reference point. It has been such people that I seem to have had an impact on.

One funny side to this is that there were some who anticipated that a negative change will most likely happen, and they wanted to help. These were probably by far the most delicate scenarios I had to negotiate, where others were trying to help me because "I needed to cope". In the first week, I was still in a hyper-excitable mood and my ego got the best of me. These early few days were challenging for me for all the wrong reasons, and I cannot overstress the importance of my community in the way I coped. These were my closest friends who I dearly love and respect, and I am very grateful that they overlooked my regrettable behaviour then.

The other change that did not take place was being engulfed with anger. I know that my forgiveness allowed me to quickly realise how strong the temptation was for me to slip down that path. Being angry and wanting to retaliate can be so easy. Coming so close to death, it is inevitable that you want to focus your anger and your hate on something. Usually, it is on the person who stabbed you. But having forgiven Ian, I never felt angry or hateful towards him, and in that, I found that I was never angry or hateful towards anyone. Others were, but not me, not my family and amazingly, not even my community. I saw the anger in others who felt victimised and angry on my behalf and I could have easily followed down that route. I also saw how some wanted to use their anger in my name.

My eyes opened up to anger and hate. I saw how it can influence people's thinking, their ideas, their words, their actions. I don't know why they felt like that, maybe it's something that was already in them, and they were just waiting, knowingly or not, for something to happen, a trigger. I think every person's response is going to be governed by their own experiences and by those who can influence them. For me, the most amazing feeling was that at no time did I feel the need to hate or to be angry. Everything

I've been doing since is in a sense to prove to people that if you can forgive, you can overcome the hate and anger within you. Not only that, but if people see you forgiving, and they believe in your forgiveness, they themselves have difficulty hating.

In fact, it is this aspect of the whole experience that I am really amazed about. You can talk all you want about theories of anger, hate, forgiveness or whatever but I've been fortunate enough to have lived it. I've seen the effect in my children, I've seen it in my family and in my friends. Someone has just stabbed your closest friend, you will be furious, angry, full of hate and aggression; they have just harmed someone you love. I've seen it in my secretaries' eyes, my friends and colleagues. Some told me that they cannot forgive him, though in time they softened their feelings. What was so revealing is the fact that the moment I forgave Ian, my entire community followed suit. Not one of them has said a bad word about Ian. From then on, all they wanted to do is to help him. How amazing is that? I have felt this, and unless you actually feel it, it is very difficult to articulate. The minute they stopped feeling anger, they started to feel sorry for him, to feel sympathetic. There is a significant transition from "I hate him", through "I don't hate him", to "I feel sorry for him" and ultimately "He needs my help." Forgiveness, to my mind, in my experience, enables that transition to take place.

But it's far from simple. I've spoken at numerous related events since, and one in particular comes to mind where I was speaking at a vigil on knife crime. I was presenting after listening to a mother who had sadly lost her son. I was getting ready to speak, but I remember feeling awkward as I could tell that those present were not anywhere near where I was. Sometimes the hurting is far too deep, and forgiveness could still feel like or come across as a betrayal to their loss. I started my presentation by saying that I felt a lot of pain that evening; everybody wanted to talk about their pain, their grievances, their loss, which is understandable, totally valid, but what they were saying never went beyond that. I felt that I needed to apologise before I spoke about forgiveness, because, I realised, they were not ready, and I was in danger of offending their grief. I said, "The minute Ian stabbed me it changed his life, and the minute I forgave him it changed my life." I then spoke about Ian as a human being and not as a criminal. I sat next to the father who had lost his son and I discovered that he was someone I had known over 12 years ago. The father had owned a restaurant, and he reminded me I'd been at his restaurant and that I'd even held his son in my hands many years ago. I asked him if he had thought about forgiveness, and he said, "Not a chance, no way." He said something close to "I'll see him in hell." But my question was not about forgiveness in the sense that you let go of what has happened, but forgiveness in the sense that you find a way to reconcile with yourself what has happened. I went to speak to mum, and as I looked at her, I could feel the pain, I saw it in her eyes. She was very polite and understanding and she knew what I was about to say, but the pain was far too overpowering. That was a very difficult moment for me, and I had to wonder about what people might understand by the word forgive.

For me forgiveness is not saying that what happened is acceptable, it never is. The harm can never be undone. Forgiving is about reconciling with yourself that you've been afflicted by a calamity, and you need to find a way to separate the pain of the calamity from the anger and hate towards the perpetrator. To me, I could see how without forgiveness the focus of the calamity remains on the perpetrator. It is focusing purely on that person who killed my son. My pain, my anger, my solace, everything is inextricably linked to what happens to the perpetrator, and in this tragic case, the law did not deliver what the heart wanted. Worse still is when you wait for an expression of remorse or an apology and it does not come. You put your own life on hold waiting for someone to let you move on. My humble feeling is that was without forgiveness there was no way for the grief to escape. Both mum and dad were grief stricken and I could do nothing to ease their pain. I hope that one day they might be able to forgive, but it's not about forgiving the person, it is forgiving your fate.

I felt then, well so much for my bloody opinion about forgiveness. But I did ask myself the question, "What would the reaction be if a son dies through an accident, through illness, through any means that cannot lead to blaming someone?" How would you cope? There is loss, there is pain, there is grief, but eventually there is some form of acceptance. Somehow, when there is someone to blame, that ultimate point of acceptance may never be achieved without the act of forgiveness. It is so confusing; you must relinquish the pain of blame to cope with the pain of loss.

In my case, I may have reached my forgiveness quickly, but I felt the impact and I am not going to be shy or reserved talking about it. I am a man of faith, and my faith is my life. As a believer, I accept that everything that happens, including a calamity, is something that Almighty God has ordained. If you accept this, if you truly believe it, then whatever happens, no matter what, even the unimaginable loss of life, it is Almighty God that you look to for answers. On a deeply personal level, the loss is between me and God. Society deals with the perpetrator in the manner society deems most appropriate. To me, forgiving the perpetrator is not forgiving the crime. On the contrary. In real terms it is refusing to let the perpetrator have any further effect on me beyond what he or she already did. It is refusing to change.

My forgiveness meant I will not be depressed, I will not be angry, I will not hate because of him. Doing so means that the perpetrator is getting from me much more than he has already taken. To me that is crazy, illogical. How can I let him control the rest of my life? My faith has given me a way to deal with such a calamity and that is to look back to Almighty God for answers. God tells me: "To heal, I need to forgive." That is the simple equation, but somehow it is just extremely difficult to do. I tell people that if you truly accept that we were born in the moment that we were allocated, and we will die in the moment that we've been allocated, and everything in between is guided by this external power that we appreciate as an Almighty God, then if you really are a true believer, whether Christian, Jewish, Muslim, Hindu, Sikh or any belief that has a similar foundation, you know that everything that happens to you is in a sense written. An act of loss, no matter how grave, is between you and your God. But it goes both ways. If something great happens to you, you should certainly be thankful to the person who has helped you, but you should also be thankful to God. That knife blade rested in my neck in an incredible place. That was also in God's hand and I must be grateful and thankful, and what better way to express that through forgiveness.

For a man like myself, reconciling my relationship with God is the key. This relationship has been developing over years, from when I was little. It was incredible that my uncle, who probably had the most influence on my relationship with God, was the first to speak to me that morning. All he did was simply remind me who I was. But what happens if you don't have such a belief? What happens if you don't have a God to turn to, even to blame? What happens if your mindset about how life works doesn't match the one that I believe in? How are you able to reconcile with what has happened? That is a more difficult one for me and I don't have an answer. I presume it is a matter of time before you submit and accept your fate. But probably by then you have given away so much of yourself and your life.

I remember that when I came back home after being at hospital, Syrsa and I talked about the incident, we didn't talk about the person. The fact that we accepted the incident, accepted that this is the way God wanted it to be, accepted that God has been merciful, this all allowed us to settle down, to reconcile. By the morning when I said I forgave Ian, I wasn't simply forgiving the person, I was expressing the fact that I had already accepted what had happened to me and there was nothing in me that felt negative. And if there was nothing negative, I think I should come out with it and say I forgive. I was just being honest about the fact that I had moved on, literally overnight. I moved on and I just kept moving on. I never looked to the person who stabbed me for answers, I never expected or waited for him to show remorse. I wasn't expecting anything from him. On the contrary, I started looking at him as one who himself needed answers, who needed to express remorse for his own sake, who needed help more than I did, and probably he even needed my help. I don't know if this is what you call forgiveness, but this is what it meant to me. And I think it all starts with reconciliation to the fact that something awful has happened. This starting point has nothing to do with the person responsible.

I have to apologise because I think I get going a bit when faith is involved. But I need to be fair here as it is not all about faith. Throughout my life I have had a debate with myself, asking should I be a proactive or a reactive person. Twenty years ago, I had no clue what this even meant, but over the years this has been a question that has occupied my mind. Gradually over the years a few incidents happened to me which taught me how to differentiate between the two. It started with one of my friends asking me the question of whether if somebody doesn't open the door for you, do you then not open the door for the next person? If you are driving and somebody does not let you through, would you then not let the next person through? He said you must ask yourself the question "Why are you opening the door in the first place?" If you're opening it because it's the right thing to do, it makes no difference if another person opens it for you. If you're opening it in response, then what other people do to you starts to make a difference. A simple dilemma, but it was the start for me. Do something because it's the right thing to do and not in response. Over the years I've worked on that principle which has come down at times to me thinking I don't want to respond, I don't need to respond, I am not going to respond. Even down to restraining myself from feeling angry, annoyed or frustrated for something done to me by another person. I try as much as I can to feel and to act according to what I think is right, and over the years I've been able to get a better hold of myself. I found that I was always at my weakest when I jump to a response. I try my best to work through my feelings and sometimes I go out of my way to respond in a different way than expected. I have tried hard to become proactive. When I was stabbed, I had to resort to these years of soul searching, but I had the fortune of doing this with my God. That's what I was doing all night, that first night. By the morning I was proactive, I had regained most of my control.

I think that my forgiveness has strengthened my relationship with my faith and my determination to remain proactive. But I also need to be fair in that my ability to forgive and to cope was made possible because of many factors. For instance, I'm not a young man and I have a few years of experience behind me. The fact that I'm involved in a faith-based community allowed me to consider these things long before the incident. I have given sermons and classes on belief, proactivity, coping and forgiveness. I think you would say that I have talked the talk. I have a good family, a good job, good colleagues, and friends. I have many things to be grateful for. I don't know if I would have been able to react in the same way without all this. I know for definite if that happened to me during my difficult years, I would have reacted completely differently. I don't think I was ready to be stabbed then!

As a measure of real change, since the incident I have noticed that the ways I think and behave are now different. I know that who I am now is not the real me. For whatever reason, I have become much more energetic, more forward and less inhibited and more than eager to express my opinion! Before, I would think twice before jumping in. Don't get me wrong, I am not shy or reserved, but I am not confrontational, not in your face, so to speak. I feel as if a burst of energy is still running through me and I have no idea where it is coming from. I know eventually it will fade, but hopefully not too soon. I am always pumped up and I am not sure what to think of it. I have become more impulsive and I seem to have the energy for it. But I am aware that it is not my normal self. Just one example was me getting involved in the phone-in debate on supporting ex-convicts to get back to work, on one of Nicky Campbell's morning shows. I would never have done this before, but following a comment made on that show, I texted back and ended up speaking on air just before I started my theatre list. It felt normal for me and I just got on with it. But being so upfront, I think that there were occasions where I could have come across as bullish and I needed to keep myself in check. That burst of energy is still with me, but I know that in time it will wane, and I will be back to my usual self. I don't think I can keep up with what I have been doing indefinitely, not with all the pressures of family and work.

Another incident was when I attended an event in Birmingham entitled The Many Faces of the Far Right. I gave a presentation on how I thought the far-right activity in my area had evolved, as well as an account of my story. There was a good discussion about how we might respond to the threat of the rising far right and I noticed how depressing the session was. It was almost as if the endgame was to resign to the fact that there was no silver lining in this cloud. By then it was 16:50 and they were just about to close the meeting. In my usual self, I would have just packed it in with everyone, but somehow, I didn't. I knew it was not my normal self, but I said to everyone in the room "Have you not listened to anything I have said?" I asked them "Look, have you ever thought about the question of whether we can in fact absorb the first blow? Somebody comes at you with their aggression and hate and you are able to absorb it and then respond in a different way?" Within just a few minutes about a third of those in the room changed their minds. I was talking about the principle of forgiveness. That was my first presentation, and what I witnessed was that the mention of forgiveness gave people hope. Despite what seemed to be a depressing and hopeless scenario, the simple consideration of forgiveness made people see the problem in a different light. The same problem, just as difficult, but a different approach, one with hope. That to me was powerful.

DT: Could you talk about some of the current work you're doing that's based around forgiveness and the consequences of your attack?

NK: Sure. As I started getting more involved, one of the things that I had difficulty deciding was where I fit. The whole experience of acting on my forgiveness is totally new to me. When I forgave Ian, I never imagined that this was going to go beyond being a personal matter. I never imagined what impact it would have on me, never mind anyone else. I must credit all those who expressed an interest in my story and who spurred me to get more involved. Coupled with that amazing energy, it just started to evolve from there. But there was a problem for me. I just did not know where my story fitted and where I could make an honest difference that was really about me and about forgiveness. That has always been my biggest fear, coming across as pretentious or phony. At the beginning I was eager to accept any invitation to get involved. I told my story a few times within the context of combating prejudice, bullying and racism. I also started to get involved in issues such as facing up to far-right narratives. I was attending seminars and events all over, using my limited spare time and leave allocation. But as this went on, I started to question myself as to where I fit. In all honesty, I still don't know. I am still waiting to see if my path is going to change again. One thing that's for sure is that if I feel an activity makes me feel positive about myself, I am more likely to do it again.

One thing that gave me a great deal of positivity was my getting involved with the Sycamore project, which initially came about from me trying to get closer to Ian. I had given up on the likelihood that I would ever be allowed to meet up with him while he was in prison and I was looking for an alternative way to get through to him, and someone mentioned the name Reverend Shawn Verhey. I managed to meet up with Reverend Verhey at Thorn Cross Prison, where he is the chaplain. He is an amazing man with endless positive energy, who ran the Sycamore programme at that low-category prison.

In brief, Sycamore is an intensive six-week programme for inmates. Its principle is restorative justice but using surrogate victims, and I've been involved with Sycamore now on three cycles (unfortunately, COVID-19 had put a big spanner in the works). Inmates subscribe to the programme, where at the end they can receive a National Vocational Qualification, so in addition to the learning and inner reflection they go through, there is also an award, a recognised certificate. This is probably the obvious carrot, but I have witnessed first-hand that some of these inmates get a great deal more than just a certificate. I have seen them break down in tears as they gradually come to terms with what they have done to their victims, to their loved ones and to themselves. The final day of the programme is immensely emotional and equally rewarding. The ultimate aim is for them not to reoffend after they leave.

I was first invited to attend the week three event where the 'surrogate' victim presents their story. I learned that they invited me to attend week three as this was when the inmates meet a victim and hear a victim's story about how the crime affected them. The inmates get to understand what they call the ripple effect of how their crime impacts many others and not just the victim, including their loved ones. They have to write this down, reflect on it and then present it in an open forum. On week six, the graduation week, they go through an open and symbolic apology where again a 'victim' is invited back. I cannot describe the feelings then, but it is very humbling, and I started looking forward to it.

Having attended for the first time just to listen, I realised that I was happy to stand in front of 20 or so inmates and just go through my experience; facing that angry man, running for my life, and then I told them about how I forgave him the following day and how I moved on. I never thought that my story would have much impact on 'hardened' inmates but the conversations that ensued were heart-warming and immensely uplifting. I realised that to simply present others with an alternative is sometimes enough for them to rethink and to reflect on their ways. Whether this had a lasting effect is not for me to say, but I felt their emotions and I saw the tears of these seemingly hardened men. On one occasion I met parents who had lost their son in a stabbing a few years ago, and I've met other Sycamore organisers who run the programme in other prisons. The impact that my story had on them was also very rewarding for me.

What amazed me most about the entire experience is the power of simply saying "I am sorry". Every inmate must stand up in front of everyone and offer a verbal apology. Some of them simply can't do it and they're allowed to either paint something, carve something, or make something to express their remorse, but a few of them wrote a poem. I've heard a few poems from these guys and unless you're there it is very difficult to give an apt description. It is fair to say that it is very moving. I'm told that usually, until week three of the programme, the engagement from the inmates is usually tentative, but from week three, there is a palpable change. It seems that coming face to face with a 'surrogate' victim has a significant impact.

Part of the exercise is for the inmates to write about an episode when they were a victim and to describe how this affected them. Reading some of the stories showed me how fragile these men were. In one such story I read about how that inmate suffered the loss of his sister who was killed. This was probably one of the most striking stories, but on the whole they were a difficult read. It's all been a big eyeopener, though the biggest impact it had on me was engaging with the prisoners themselves. You can never excuse what they have done and the harm they have inflicted, but they are there in prison, serving their time, and through Sycamore they are making an effort, some of them definitely, and you can tell.

I sat talking to one of them on my first attendance. We made contact as he had previously broken his ankle and we started talking about that. He had a drug-addiction problem and he knew that his problem would be there when he was released. Sadly, this inmate passed away a few weeks later and I managed to attend and to speak at his funeral. Being involved with Sycamore is hopefully going to be one of the long-term commitments for me. Something related I would love to do is to see if I can be involved with these inmates after their release. I don't know how realistic this is but if the opportunity arises, I will most likely take it.

Another activity that developed over the past two years is my presentations to secondary schoolchildren on the power of forgiveness. I have now given the presentation over a dozen times with on occasions over 200 students attending. The PowerPoint presentation is interactive and takes the students through my story followed by the potential response and how fear, depression and anger can lead to resentment and hate, and how this can ultimately pave the way to violence. I then tell them about my forgiveness and how this empowered me not to hate or seek revenge, but to heal and seek reconciliation. At the end of the presentation, I take a pledge with the students to replace ignorance with knowledge, fear with courage, hate with understanding and violence with forgiveness. I have had very positive feedback at these presentations

This is something that I will carry on doing until I am far too old to be there, but I am very happy that I am able to have an impact on the young. Whenever I give a presentation on forgiveness, at the end of the meeting I always ask those present who among them is prepared to forgive. Initially, there is silence but gradually you see a hand going up, and then another. It is not easy to forgive, and it is not something that is instinctive in people's minds. I believe that through my presentation, at least I am offering an alternative that someone might benefit from sometime in their life.

DT: It is clear that forgiveness fortified you and your family, helped you to deal with the situation. Were there aspects to the ensuing situation that nevertheless still felt pressured, difficult to negotiate, even perhaps *because* you had adopted that position, those community members doubting you, for instance?

NK: When speaking about the influence of forgiveness on my behaviour and thinking, I have tended to focus mainly on the early phase where my forgiveness allowed me and my family to cope with the immediate fallout of such a traumatic event. But there is something that I argued about with Syrsa and I think is also part of that hidden change, the change that never took place. After what happened in the first couple of days, we also had to cope with public opinion, the police, the CPS, the criminal justice system, and eventually meeting Ian's family. I mentioned earlier about the deep painful impact on the victim and their loved ones when the law does not deliver. Getting back to work, having that buzz, being proactive, little of that prepares you to cope with the bigger picture. I will give you examples.

As soon as I was stabbed, everyone assumed it was a hate-motivated attack, what else could it have been? Everyone was horrified that this was a targeted attack on the grounds of a mosque. At least the police will investigate this possibility to the hilt. There was, however, another assumption by many in my community that because we are Muslims, the investigation will be a token gesture, if not a whitewash, and so on. I read through the Stephen Lawrence case and I read through what happened to the defendants in the Bradford riots. At the beginning, I read a lot about the law, charges, what constitutes a hate crime and a hate incident. I even corresponded with experts and professors on this topic to see where my crime fitted. The bottom line is that I was getting that deep sense of injustice based on historical events and perceptions. When the charges were announced, everyone was telling me this is an outrage, it was the whitewash they expected. Where is the justice in that? These were genuine feelings expressed by others that Syrsa and I had to deal with, as well as dealing with our own feelings. The two of us had so many arguments together and this spurred us more to look and read further into something that we knew virtually nothing about. But by then, the police had no more interest in my story. It felt for us that it was all wrapped up. Well, how do you deal with such thoughts and such emotions?

Even worse, there were some that said to me, "Well we did tell you so", or "why did you forgive?" Some even suggested that my forgiveness paved the way for the police to be even more relaxed and blasé about my case. In their minds, it was as if it was about their case. Because I am a

Muslim, it is not just about me, it is about everyone like me. These feelings of victimisation ran deep, especially the fact that, at the time, Islamophobic hate incidents and crimes were on the rise in Manchester. Only a few weeks earlier a mosque suffered an arson attack in North Manchester. The perpetrators were never caught and the impression I was given was that this did not even get to the news. It seemed to be another whitewash, because it was Muslims, and in that particular case it was a double whammy, in that they were mostly black Muslims. So, you see, the general mood was there for me to feel victimised, to feel enraged and to engage with how others felt, how they wanted me to feel.

The first thing that happened because of forgiveness was that no one could speak on my behalf. That was incredibly powerful. But the other thing that happened was the effect it had on me and my wife. When we started to research and build up our information, we were non-judgemental in the way we saw things. Between the two of us, we were always arguing the case for and the case against any perception. We argued the charge, we argued the hate aspect, we argued the extent of my injury and how the police would see it. We even started to give the police excuses. We argued sometimes nicely and sometimes fiercely. I remember that on occasions we ended up shouting at each other because we saw it so differently.

To me, that is another hidden change of forgiveness. It was not plain sailing, it was painful, it was the pain of accepting what is real and ditching the comfort of perceptions. Our arguments were not easy. There were moments when we got angry, got frustrated, felt let down and felt excluded from our own case, but we were able to argue ourselves to what you might call common sense. Forgiveness allowed us to see the common sense. Of course, common sense is not perfect, that is the whole point. It did not have to be perfect, it is never perfect, but it made sense. These were very difficult feelings that we had to deal with day in, day out. And we were able to see our way through them. Until the trial was finished, we had to try very hard to overcome the feelings of mistrust that we had towards the police and the CPS. I found out how easy it was to get that them-and-us feeling. To trust the police and the legal system was viewed as naïve, stupid. I must be honest, those feelings kept on surfacing, but we had to overcome it otherwise it would have driven us crazy.

It was difficult, but we saw our way through all that and I honestly think it was because we saw the process as not about us. I presume this is what forgiveness gives you. You can negotiate your feelings about injustice, or the perception of injustice, the fact that the legal system is there for the person who nearly killed me, but it was not there for me. This I think was one of the most difficult feelings to deal with.

If I am brutally honest, in that context, I think that forgiveness allowed me to retain my sanity when I could have easily been carried away with everyone's emotions, including my own. We endured that period of uncertainty and by the end of the legal process, we felt that we dealt with the them-and-us in an honest way, which eventually led us to cope with the whole legal process better. I know full well that the legal process can never be perfect. It is impossible for it to be perfect. I am a doctor and I know that any system that depends on people can never be perfect; it is only as good as its people.

As a professional, I have no doubt that errors were made in my case. It is impossible for errors not to happen. When I went through the trial, I spotted so many errors, but to me they reflected the professionalism of the process and not an intention to undermine the fact that someone nearly killed me. My forgiveness allowed me and Syrsa to see it for what it is, and not for what our emotions wanted us to believe. I honestly think that this is by far the most personally powerful aspect of forgiveness. It is the ability to cope with the imperfections of life without thinking that you are still being victimised. The system is not perfect, but it is not because of who you are.

Now someone will say "Hold on a minute, what about institutional racism?" I know that I have not faced that, so it will be difficult for me to give a meaningful answer. Sometimes you need to carry some grief and pain with you to seek the truth just like what happened in the Stephen Lawrence case. The people who have done that are far stronger than I could ever be. But once justice has been achieved, you still need to forgive. You need to heal.

DT: How do you think someone might embed some of the ideas this book has discussed, of being proactive and of forgiving, in everyday circumstances?

NK: I don't know, I mean I look at my children and of course like any parent I wonder how I can influence their thinking positively. The truth is I can't, or rather it is not that simple. People are all different, different ages, backgrounds, beliefs and so on. How can you relay a message that is the same for everyone? That's something I have struggled with. I know that leadership is important, but this means setting an example, and from my experience, I know that there is a limit to what setting an example can achieve. This is very difficult because people's experiences are so different.

So, for me, what it boils down to is something that I truly believe in. The starting point is that you need to be comfortable with yourself. If you are not, I think it will be more difficult to accept what life throws at you. In order to be proactive and forgiving, and hopefully resilient in difficult circumstances, it has to start with you being a person that is comfortable with yourself. When something bad happens, a misfortune or whatever, if you're not comfortable with yourself, and you're angry with yourself, with your life or your circumstances, it's very difficult to respond appropriately, to be proactive, to be forgiving.

Exploring the idea of forgiveness is really about asking how to make someone feel comfortable and happy with their own existence. That fundamentally is my problem when talking about forgiveness. It is not an equal starting point for everyone. It took me years to be comfortable with my own existence. I wasn't happy with my existence 20 years ago, 30 years ago. But then, even though I was not happy with my life, by my nature, I'm not a person who gets angry quickly. I get frustrated, but not necessarily angry. Interestingly, when I was living on my own, I was more likely to get frustrated than angry. After getting married, I found myself getting angry more easily, probably driven by the responsibility of a family.

Anyway, I am also the sort of person that doesn't blame anyone else for the difficulties I had when I was younger. I never really tried to blame anyone else, and I think that is probably one of my biggest assets, but how can you teach that? If I was going through a difficulty, I always looked to myself for the solution rather than focusing on another person to apportion blame to or to solve the situation for me. This made me more aware of my own failings and helped me work on them. I always tended to ask myself what I could do to get myself out of a situation. I think if there is one thing that I would wish others to believe in, it is the idea: don't focus on others, your strength comes from within you. People who have overcome difficulties, people who are successful, tend to do that, they look to themselves for answers.

Getting back to the question, to be able to be proactive and be able to forgive, it starts with accepting who you are, with first looking inwards for answers and possibly to have a good role model. For me, as a man of faith, probably more accurately an old man of faith, I found my relationship with God allowed me to be more accepting of the bad things in my life.

DT: I know we've spoken about it a bit, but nevertheless I want to ask the direct question of whether you believe it is possible to encourage others to forgive, given that this way you're describing it means it needs someone to be stable in themselves first, but you can't plan for that, and at moments of disaster and tragedy then understandably someone might be at their least stable?

NK: The answer is no, much as I would like the answer to be yes. I've learnt in life that forgiveness is not a passive response; forgiveness is a very proactive and active response. It isn't something that can happen just like that. It's a process which may entail years of agony, years of soul searching. But this, of course, is my own personal experience. We have an example in medicine that may explain this better. We have the term "a diagnosis by exclusion". This is the sort of diagnosis that cannot be reached in its own right. It can only be reached by having excluded everything else. When the situation is so overwhelming, forgiveness is probably not the first thing that comes to mind. But through a painful process, it is likely that the person will come to that inevitable conclusion: "To heal, I need to forgive." You probably go through all sorts of emotions and reactions, but none will give you the answer that will calm your heart. So, for me, it is not whether you forgive early that is the issue; it is finding forgiveness somewhere along the journey. No doubt, the sooner you do, the less of your life you have wasted.

I can never know what is going through a parent's mind after losing a child. The loss, the agony, the guilt, the anger, the grief, and so much more. Sometimes the raging anger inside that parent can be a way to lessen the pain of loss. That pain is unimaginable, and you need to find something to cope with that pain. It might be that you want to forgive, but the pain can only be reduced by anger. That parent is not ready. It is just too painful to be ready to forgive. At the beginning, there might not even be hate, just anger. But I have seen a problem with that. Anger is never a long-term solution. The anger that is there masking the pain, by its nature will never let the pain go away. The initial coping mechanism becomes itself the problem. On top of that, that ongoing anger opens up the door for resentment and hate. In the right setting, it is a recipe for something awful.

We should not underestimate how difficult it is to forgive, for many reasons. But we should not confuse an inability to forgive with meaning that someone does not want to forgive. We have to accept that they may not be ready. Deep inside they may want to forgive but they don't have what it takes to do so by themselves. Yes, ultimately forgiveness is a personal act, but you need others with you to help you do so. Also, the inability to forgive does not mean that there is hate for the other person, but if you are not careful, it can end up that way. In short, it's not that people don't want to forgive, but you need the ability, you need support, and you need time.

In my experience, I've gone through a good deal of painful experiences in my past, though probably no more than average. But I am fortunate to say that I overcame them. Some of these difficulties lasted over a number of years, but eventually there was light at the end of that tunnel. When you go through such an experience, it tells you that you always need to be hopeful. You cannot simply give up. You cannot be the reason for your own failing. When I look back at those years, I never regretted the fact that I went through them, but at the time it didn't feel that way at all. In some sense, I have felt both sides of the coin. When I was going through the pain, I could not see an end, but I think if you go through something like that in your life it just gives a different perspective on things.

With my outlook on life, and when it comes to a great loss, I would almost go as far as saying that forgiveness is necessary. I have had the sad privilege of meeting two sets of parents who have both lost a child. One had forgiven and one was struggling to forgive. I have seen both and I know who needed to heal, badly. The pain was the same, the grief was the same. But one set of parents were still trapped and needing; the other have become free to help others.

DT: Might we explore a little the idea of forgiveness being to do with an acceptance of an inevitability of all things?

NK: Great question. Can I first make the assumption that "acceptance of the inevitability of all things" means accepting fate? If so, for me I have always seen fate as an integral part of my faith. If you do not believe in God, in creation that is, then what else do you hang on to explain this "inevitability"? What is the logic of this "inevitability"? Trying to get your head round this one can drive you mad. Why is your inevitability better or worse than someone else's? If it is indeed so, and in our lives it definitely is, why should you accept that fate?

So far, I have not been able to get my head round this one. My debates with friends of no faith never get us round this one. But it is not simply about faith, as I know for sure that there are many people of faith who simply are not able to forgive. I am still searching for an answer, but I'm going to tell you something interesting for me. I recently bumped into a lady while on the Sycamore programme who did the same work, but at a different prison. I don't know how it came about, but I did ask her if she had come across anyone who does not have a religion-based faith and yet was able to forgive, and she said yes. For me, that was an exciting moment and I want to explore it further. I'm hoping to meet this person one day because I really want to look deeper into that.

If I am going to be honest to the idea of forgiveness, I need to be fair and openminded. My own experience could be just what it is, only my own experience. Forgiveness in its truest form may have little to do with faith. The conversation I had that day was an eyeopener for me. I needed to know how you reach an acceptance of forgiveness when you have no faith. I obviously still don't know, but I can have a guess.

It is probably that we tend to mix up the words faith and religion and use them interchangeably. For me, they may relate but they are definitely not the same. I don't want to put words into anyone's mouth, but many people say that they don't have a faith when they mean they don't have a religion. I do have to accept that this is what I think, and it may not be totally true, but I have seen it. Many who state that they do not have a faith, have not come to the definite conclusion that there is no greater entity out there. For instance, when you can't explain everything in your life, and even if you do not have a religion, you will eventually resign yourself to feeling that there is a greater power out there, you just don't know what it is. That is what I think, but probably this is just me rambling on.

Anyhow, that conversation again made me question my understanding of the relationship of faith to an act of forgiveness. In my own my case, my belief in God and my understanding of Islam have provided me with a practical method. When I was in my bed that first night after the stabbing, I knew I could lie there and speak to my God on my own. I understood from my faith that I can do that. In fact, I have been doing that on a daily basis throughout my life. I questioned God, I spoke to God, I was unsure of God's purpose and so on. Yes, for some this may sound utterly crazy, if not downright stupid. However, ultimately, I resigned my fate and my judgment to God, and this is essentially my coping mechanism. Does that mean that this is proof that God exists? Absolutely not! But what it means without a shadow of doubt is that such a coping mechanism is just about the strongest that exists. This is no longer as crazy or as stupid as it may have appeared.

As a doctor, I am not foreign to thinking about the ethics and psychology of behaviour. In a clinical setting, God does not really feature. The psychology of behaviour is a science in its own right: how to cope, how to be positive, how to be successful, how to understand and deal with bias and prejudice. Not only that, but now the science also includes a better understanding of the circuitry in our brains and the chemicals involved, the serotonin, dopamine, endorphins and the like. We can now easily change someone's mood through medication. I am sure our coping mechanisms, our ability to be positive and probably our ability to forgive will depend on certain circuitry and certain chemicals in our brains. This seems to be logical. In my humble personal opinion, it is my belief that God has created this brain of ours to work in a certain way, and I have been taught through my religion how to best use it. I'm sure that without a faith, it is still possible to figure out how this brain of ours works and we will eventually come to the conclusion that forgiveness is most likely the logical thing to do. This logic does not necessarily require a faith or a God. For me, I was able to reach that logic just through faith.

DT: One question I have is the same question I might put to someone with or without faith, which is do you think there is anything that is unforgivable?

NK: Perhaps the answer is already in your question. Your question is do I think there is "anything" that is unforgivable, you didn't ask do I think there is "anybody" who is unforgivable, and I think the two are totally different. There is no act which is forgivable. I don't forgive acts; it's not for us to forgive acts. I forgive a person, and I honestly think in my mind the two are completely separate. There is no forgiving for stabbing a knife in anybody's neck; this is unforgivable, but the person who's done it, that's a different story.

So, no evil act of whatever sort, as an act, there is no way on earth I would condone such an act whatsoever by forgiving it; this is silly. It is never about forgiving the act. It is about forgiving the person. So, the question could be "Can you forgive a person doing anything?" You see, once you start looking at the person committing the act, you take a different perspective than when you purely think of the act itself. Now, there are evil acts that are committed by one person and there are acts that are committed by a small gang, or by a larger organisation, but most frightening, there are evil acts committed by a nation. For the extreme example of this, people often refer to acts of genocide. The Holocaust, Cambodia, Rwanda, Bosnia are just a few. Is any of that forgivable, is anyone forgivable?

You don't have to ask me this question, ask someone who has been affected. Ask a Jewish person about forgiveness and the Holocaust and you will hear amazing and humbling answers. I'm not Jewish, so I am not in a position to comment on the Holocaust. But as a Muslim I can comment on the genocide in Bosnia. As with all these atrocities, it is not just the genocide, but also the rapes and all the other associated crimes and atrocities. Was that forgivable? Is any of it forgivable? Is anyone involved forgivable? I have already said that not one evil act is ever forgivable. So, we are now talking about the perpetrators. But hold on a minute, even as a Muslim considering the genocide in Bosnia, who the hell am I to even consider if anyone is forgivable? It needs to be stated without any qualifications: no one, absolutely no one has the right to forgive on behalf of anyone else's suffering. Forgiveness is one of the most humane acts that one can do. For it to be honest and pure, it has to be done willingly and from the depth of one's heart. It doesn't even have to be openly expressed, it can remain in one's heart, where that person alone knows it is there. That should be our starting point. Only then can you start unravelling these unspeakable atrocities down to individual actions by individual people. Literally every action and every person. When you do that, it starts to take on a different perspective, but unless you do that, it will be impossible to reach an understanding.

This is in fact one of the absolute Islamic principles: no one person is held responsible for the action of another. Once we see it that way, there is then the need for each and every person that has been harmed to seek within themselves, should they choose to do so, to forgive that person or persons who have caused their pain and suffering. This will include every mother who has lost her husband and children, every woman and girl who has been raped, and everyone else who has endured a suffering of whatever kind in this atrocity. That is what forgiveness demands. I know sometimes it is easier to forgive when a group of victims come together to heal as a group and they forgive as a group, but even then, they can only forgive what has happened to them individually.

You have asked me a very difficult question, and as you can see, the complexity of my answer is probably my way of wriggling out of committing myself to an answer. But with such horrendous atrocities, how can you ever see your way through all this? Such an atrocity is simply too horrific to even contemplate forgiveness, it almost seems as if I am belittling the atrocity by even suggesting that forgiveness is a remote possibility. Well, probably you don't have to, or you don't need to forgive; you just move on with others with your pain. You move on knowing that the source of that pain has now stopped. But for many, they just cannot move on and they get trapped in their pain, anger and grief, like those parents of the murdered son. What is left for them? Well, maybe the only option is that of forgiveness, but just as I said in another answer, it is also not simply about forgiving the person, it is about forgiving your fate. I am sure that this is as clear as mud.

But there is another principle in Islam, and it is the understanding that everything is forgivable in the sight of

God, if you believe in God that is. But such forgiveness has principles. For God to forgive a heinous crime, there are four steps demanded. The first is recognition of one's crime and accepting the legal punishment and recompense. The second is to stop the wrongdoing. The third is a recognition that what was done is wrong and expressing regret and remorse. Finally, a genuine desire and commitment never to do that again. These are the conditions in Islam when seeking repentance and the forgiveness of God. I've spoken about this in my sermons. On a personal level, the message is that God has opened the door for repentance and for forgiveness to everyone, irrespective of what they have done, but given the four conditions.

So how can that be the case, and is it for any crime? The truth is that Islam drives the understanding that by default human nature is weak, very weak. We should never look down at sinners and we should never gloat, saying they are sinners and, thereby, I am the better person. We are asked to consider the fact that "I am fortunate that I have not been put in a position where I could have been that sinner." The mindset here is one of being thankful for the fact that you are not born into or raised in an environment that leads you to be part of that evil. I know I still have not answered your question, but I hope I have given you something to think about.

That said, there is another angle to this. When I try to explain forgiveness, I focus mainly on the ability to cope with the harm that has been caused to the victim. But what can you say in the case of rape or paedophilia? Can you ever ask if anyone can forgive rape or paedophilia? I think the question in its own right is derogatory. This is where I get worried about my line of thinking on more than one level. How can you separate the act from the perpetrator in such a case?

These people are evil, aren't they? What about society? What message does forgiveness give when the crime is of that nature? It is too sensitive, too muddy. I don't believe that when it comes to the question of forgiveness here, that there can be a personal or individual point of view. Society must step in to support the victim, to help them cope and deal with their tragic ordeal. But even then, one of the answers the victim may seek is how to reconcile with what had happened to them with their fate. In fact, let me throw the question back at you. Is it forgivable that a person who has been wronged so badly, that their life should come to a standstill? For this is exactly what can happen. Society needs to be proactive in supporting these victims to get their lives back. Does forgiveness play a role? I honestly don't know. And even then, I don't have the right to express anything other than an individual opinion. I don't know if you think that this is a cop out.

So, getting back to the question, is anything forgivable? I would answer back, is it necessary to forgive? If the victim can overcome and can heal from their ordeal and can get back into their lives as best as they can without having to forgive, then you have your answer. I think I would leave it at that. We need to be careful not to sound as if forgiveness is an easy option or the only option. This may end up coming across as if not much thought is given to just how evil man can be. It might even come across as belittling and undermining the unimaginable atrocity that a victim has suffered. There needs to be a sensitive approach here and we need to consider what we are trying to achieve through forgiveness. Yet the hard questions remain: how can we help the victim to move on, or even to want to move on?

When considering forgiveness, it is not just about what it is to be forgiven. It is also about who can forgive. As I said before, I cannot forgive on anyone else's behalf. So, if your question is for me personally, then most likely yes, I would be prepared to forgive anything that happens to me. But I cannot project my answer onto others. That is not acceptable. In fact, it is condescending. To be honest, and having though about it, even when I answer "Yes" myself it can still come across as condescending. The truth is that I will try my best to be forgiving and to be compassionate, because I know this is the only way for me to move on with my life. I hope that if ever I had to face such a question, that I can find the answer for myself again.

Your question is actually something that I have thought about since that fateful day. When I've been asked to present my story in a setting where I felt that the other victims present are not ready to consider forgiveness, I feel that I don't have the right to talk about my forgiveness. I downplay my role and provide an alternative narrative. In the vigil about knife crime, I said, "I'm going to introduce you to the person who stabbed me" and I said "his father was an alcoholic", "he had mental health issues, he is on medication". I said things like, "the mental health system has failed him, society has failed him, and he has failed himself", and I tell them that my crime was years in the making; it didn't just happen on that day. This was me trying to get them to think not just about the crime, but about themselves, about what has happened to them, what happened to the perpetrator, telling them that there's more than one victim here. Just trying to give another perspective to the crime, getting them to think in a different way. On days like that I can really feel like I'm on thin ice, asking myself what the relevance is of my bloody forgiveness to what has happened to this family. These situations make me feel really awkward, but I would be doing the wrong thing if I at least did not introduce the angle of forgiveness. If in such a setting I am ever asked about the idea that everything is forgivable, I would say that it is something that is not up to me to answer. Each victim has to answer the question for themselves.

DT: I wonder whether you think that forgiveness might in some way be connected with redemption? I suppose I am thinking of it in quite simplistic ways really. My starting query is whether some form of redemption can be possible without forgiveness?

NK: Just take me through that again please and tell me what redemption means to you?

DT: I mean some sort of equivalent or at least comparable reconciliation with events, that is a perpetrator finding a way to some stable path, similar to that which you're talking about that a victim might find.

NK: I see. This is really a very nice question. In short, I am not sure. The answer I think is not straightforward; probably it is more difficult to find redemption without forgiveness. But first, there is a judicial process to consider. A crime has been committed, the judicial process is involved, and the guilty person receives their punishment. So, you may ask has the judicial process helped the perpetrator to find redemption? They may have reflected on their guilt, on the time of their life wasted in prison and on other things but is that finding redemption? Possibly not. You see, in real terms, that is what the judicial system has to offer, and I don't think that the redemption you are referring to can be achieved through that. In fact, so many people leave prison only to reoffend, so where is the redemption in that? The judicial process is society's accepted way of dealing with crime. It is not designed to support the victim and it is not designed for the purpose of offender redemption. You need to look elsewhere, if that is what you are looking for.

In any case, to begin any process of redemption, the perpetrator needs to want to do so, he needs to face up to his crime, to understand the harm and hurt he caused not just to the victim of his crime but to everyone else, including his own loved ones. A prison sentence does not necessarily do that by itself. The punishment of a prison sentence may in fact have the opposite effect. The criminal may think that he has served his debt to society, so why is there a need for anything else? The sad reality is that the same may also be viewed by society. The criminal has served his dues, so what right does society have to expect him to seek redemption? I hope I am making sense here. This is probably where something like the Sycamore programme comes in.

I don't know what Ian is thinking now. He has been given his sentence and hopefully I may be able to meet him someday. However, I can't predict what he would do. Having met the inmates at Thorn Cross, everyone is different. They're all individual in their own way. They all have their own problems and shortcomings. As we are coming to the end of the book, I can say that Ian and I have only very recently spoken on the phone. We will see what develops from that.

However, getting back to your question, for now I can only express an opinion based on what I have witnessed through the Sycamore programme. This is why I think that if redemption is possible it will need forgiveness. But there are a few things to consider. Again, we go back to the starting point. There is a need to face up to one's crime and to want to change. In my limited experience and from what I have seen with the inmates, many of them have never come across an act of forgiveness, or at least not one they remember. They have no idea how to forgive or even how to respond if someone forgives them. They are, on the surface, hardened and tough men. For them forgiveness is a weakness. This is where forgiveness expressed by the victim can be so powerful. It hits these seemingly tough men in their weakest spot. This was my experience when I tell them that I have forgiven the person that stabbed me. The first thing they say is "How could you?" But when I tell them about the strength of forgiveness, this is when they start to believe it. Not all of them of course. But for me, that is usually good enough. I hope that once they believe in forgiveness, they may start reconsidering what they want to do. Will that lead to redemption? I really don't know, and I need to be realistic, but there is no harm in hoping.

The other thing that I think about is whether the offer of forgiveness can be conditional. This is something that I find difficult. Yes, it may sound like a good idea. For me, I still feel that forgiveness is a selfless act, offered without conditions. It is offered with hope. That is what makes it genuine and powerful. In a way, withholding forgiveness is almost like saying to the perpetrator, I will not give you the chance for redemption; you don't deserve it. That is a horrible thought and why would we do that?

There is one last angle to redemption that I would like to consider, on a personal level. I myself have caused harm to others throughout the years. Like everyone else, I've done some bad things. So, where do I seek my own redemption for what I have done? I know I've hurt people in the past and before I had the chance to seek their forgiveness, we went our separate ways. I've not seen them again and probably I never will. I sometimes wonder how could I make this up to someone who I have hurt? I take some comfort in thinking that my willingness to forgive gives me hope that others in turn may find it in their heart to forgive me. It is not just about realising redemption. It is also about the hope of redemption.

Ripples: Family & Friends

The following contributions are from Dr Kurdy's family, friends and colleagues. They are included as a way of giving voices to those affected indirectly, if we can call it indirectly, by the events surrounding the stabbing; they are the kinds of "ripple" effects of an act of violence that the programmes Dr Kurdy is involved in within prisons focus upon. The contributions also illustrate how difficult it can be to remember everything around the events of a traumatic event accurately: the phone call to Syrsa; the things said upon arrival in the mosque's hall, for example. These events are recalled slightly differently by different people. Given that this book has questioned the efficacy of certain legal processes, we thought it fair to include such alternative recollections, but, just as importantly, such differences tell of how such "ripples" are unpredictable and individual.

Syrsa Kurdy

It was a Sunday and Nasser was in the garden sorting out the flowerbeds. Suddenly I saw him hurrying back in to have a shower and he mentioned that he had a meeting at the mosque. As he left, I carried on with the hoovering. All of a sudden, my mobile was ringing but at the same time, there was banging on the front door and the doorbell went. It all happened at the same time and I remember not knowing whether to answer the phone first or the door. I picked up the phone and went to open the door. It was Nasser on the phone, and Baji Shahnaz with Saima Alvi at the door. Nasser told me he was going to A&E but that he felt well, and he did sound OK to me on the phone which reassured me as the looks on both Shahnaz and Saima's faces were very alarming. They said that something very serious had taken place and took me to the living room. Despite what they were saying, I felt unusually calm. As they went through what had taken place, I wasn't paying attention so much to what was being said but I was focusing more on the fact that I felt safe in my heart. They asked me if I wanted to go to the hospital and it was only then that I realised that our son Oaiss had left just a few minutes ago. I said that I needed to make sure that Oaiss got back first to be with our other son Ahmad before I could leave. Ahmad at the time was playing on his computer. I phoned Oaiss and reassured him as to what had happened and asked him to come back. I told Ahmad that his dad was OK, I had just spoken to him and he sounded fine. I did my afternoon prayers and Saima drove me to the hospital.

When I got to the hospital, I noticed a few friends were already there in the waiting area and I sat with them. I remember a policeman speaking to Saima but still I was not concentrating on what was being said. It sounded as if this was a targeted attack on the mosque but that 'very likely' by tomorrow the attacker would be deemed as having a mental-health problem, but not as a terrorist. This was the gist of what I heard. A few minutes later Nasser was brought back from his scan. He was his usual self, joking that his head scan confirmed he did have a brain after all. They took me in to be with him and the two of us were alone. I asked him what happened, and he said he needed to concentrate on what the man who attacked him said exactly. He told me the policeman had already asked him about that and he needed to calm down and try and recall exactly what was said to him, without anyone's interfering. He had his eyes closed trying to remember what the man said. A few minutes later the policeman came back and requested Nasser's trousers, shirt, belt and even demanded the shoes and Nasser started to undress. At that time, I said all praise be to Almighty God

(Alhamdullilah), he has shown us so much of His mercy. I left the emergency room and went out to the waiting area to ask a friend to fetch some clothes for Nasser. I mentioned that Oaiss was at home and should be able to help with that. By then I was reassured about the physical and emotional state of my husband. I felt calm and felt the blessing of Almighty God. I was no longer thinking of what might be going on with regards to the man who stabbed Nasser, or why he did it or what my friends were focused on. These things did not seem to matter to me anymore. Within the next half an hour, Nasser was on his feet walking with the help of one of our friends, Dr Akeel, leaving the hospital. Dr Akeel's sister is a friend of over 25 years and she was also there with him. He drove us home that evening. As he left, he told us to rest, but by then both of us were feeling relaxed and peaceful. Back at home, our daughter Assma phoned us from Spain, and she spoke to her dad and was reassured that he was safe and sound. Oaiss and Ahmad were also both reassured when they saw him walking in and by then Oaiss said that there were already comments circulating on social media. I remember that they both said something about sending a message, but I wasn't concentrating on what they were saying. I do, however, remember that I felt it to be a calm and peaceful evening and when I look back on that evening at home, when Nasser and I sat together speaking and when we spoke to the children, and we kept on saying that there was a divine wisdom in what had taken place, I recall that we felt blessed and we were not angry or depressed or hateful. All that we felt was acceptance and contentment with what had happened. It seemed that each of us felt the same.

A few friends phoned to make sure we were OK, after which we all went to bed. I remember that despite the painkiller Nasser had, I noticed he was tossing and turning in bed every time I opened my eyes. I don't think he slept at all that night. I was sure that the wound was deep and very painful. At 7 in the morning, we woke up to a phone call from Nasser's uncle in Damascus. I think they spoke for about 15 minutes. I went downstairs and prepared coffee and got Ahmad ready for school. It felt very peaceful that morning at home and it was as if nothing had taken place the previous evening except for the fact that as I opened the front door, the press was already there. As I drove off to school, I phoned Saima and told her that the press was standing outside our house and asked her if she would be able to get to our home.

I dropped off Ahmad at school, and I felt that he was his normal self and was feeling OK. When I got back home, Saima was already there and was speaking with the press. All I did then was prepare them coffee, tea and biscuits and I was somehow playing the incident down. It seems that this did not work as every half hour another press team kept showing up.

Assma Kurdy

I was in Barcelona the day I found out about dad's stabbing. I was watching a movie with friends in our Airbnb apartment when my brother, Oaiss, called me. I thought it was strange for him to be calling me whilst I was abroad, so I went to another room to answer. I vaguely remember the conversation; him saying that there was something he needed to tell me but being very clear that I was not to panic and repeating this, multiple times. Of course, I started panicking. When he told me that dad had been stabbed in the neck outside a mosque, I felt faint and had to sit down. My voice must have been loud because it alerted my friends that something was wrong. So many thoughts were running through my head: Should I book a ticket and go back to Manchester immediately? How was mum coping? What happened exactly? Did they catch the perpetrator? Oaiss told me that my dad was alive and OK, so although I continued to feel on edge, I was not delirious. When I told my friends, they were shocked, but they were very supportive and calming. Within a few minutes I received the first of many kind messages. It began with "I'm sorry to hear about your dad". At that moment I was grateful to my brother for calling me and giving me the heads up. In hindsight I realised that receiving a message starting with "I'm sorry to hear about your dad" with no context would have worried me much more than his phone call.

Shortly after speaking to my brother, my mum called to reassure me that she was with my dad and he was in a stable condition. I remember them joking over the phone which made me feel better. They told me not to worry about coming back straight away and to enjoy the rest of my holiday. I did somehow manage to enjoy the last two days of the holiday, with the lingering thought of my dad and family at the back of my mind. I was anxious to see them.

After arriving back in London, I caught a train to Manchester immediately. I remember getting home and feeling astonished at how normal my family were. I was a little worried they had been putting on a brave voice for my sake, but they really were very composed and relaxed. My parents' conviction in God and belief that everything happens for a reason really resonated with me, and to me, this is why they were able to remain level-headed throughout the ordeal and its aftermath.

In the immediate aftermath of the stabbing, the support we received from extended family, friends, the community and strangers was extremely heart-warming. Dad received hundreds of cards and letters of well-wishes, many of which were from his patients. I hadn't appreciated before this point how much of an impact my dad's service as a doctor had on people's lives. I remember logging into Facebook and seeing articles posted about my dad by major news outlets. I scrolled through hundreds of comments posted by kind strangers, again some of whom had been his patients. I showed him some of these in excitement because they made me feel so happy. Over the next few days my dad was interviewed numerous times by different media outlets. It was very strange to see him on national news, but I felt proud and also very relieved that he was well enough to be at home to do these interviews.

I can't remember at exactly which point I found out that the police had apprehended the attacker, but I was extremely relieved when I found out. The thought of this person roaming the streets freely made me very anxious. Because dad was so forgiving of the situation, I realise now that his attitude subconsciously affected my emotions as I can't recall ever feeling angry at the attacker. At most, I was curious about his motivations. Was he Islamophobic? Was he simply mentally unstable? If anything, I was more taken aback by my parents' response to the incident than the incident itself, so I wasn't very consumed with thoughts about this mystery man.

The court proceedings and eventual trial seemed to drag on for a very long time. I really wanted to be there physically with my family but could not attend as my work is based in London. I was not satisfied with the ultimate decision as the attacker was found not guilty of attempted murder, which I thought was ludicrous given that the stabbing was in the neck! The experience was eye-opening to say the least. Having studied law, I already knew that the burden of proof favoured the defendant, but it can be a difficult pill to swallow when a loved one is involved. My brothers also explained that the defence lawyer was particularly persuasive and charming, so they were not surprised with the outcome. I remember them amusingly describing how they tried to decipher which way the jury would vote (and they were right). Ultimately the lawyer you are assigned by the Crown Prosecution Service is an exercise in luck, but I found it interesting that something as trivial as a lawyer's style of speech might ultimately swing a jury's decision.

Despite his not being convicted of attempted murder, I am relieved that the attacker was found guilty of a number of other offences and has served a lengthy jail sentence. Part of this relief stems from the fact that he has not been roaming the streets with the potential intention of doing this to someone else. However, having learned that he has had a difficult upbringing and suffers from some mental-health issues, I do also hope that he receives the help and rehabilitation he needs. At the end of the day my dad is alive and well, he has forgiven this man for what he did and if anything has expressed sympathy towards him, so how can I not wish the same for him? I would be lying if I said that I would be this eager to forgive him if the outcome had been different; God forbid if my dad had suffered permanent damage, or even worse, had been killed.

Throughout this experience I have felt so proud of dad. I cannot recall how many times someone has brought him up to me in conversation, asking about how he's doing, telling me how impressed they were by his response and letting me know how inspiring he has been. An Islamic principle we live by is that God does not burden a soul more than it can bear. For this reason, in a strange way I am glad this test was chosen for my dad as I'm not sure anyone else could have turned this disturbing incident into a message of positivity the way he has. He has a specific demeanour and way with words that makes him very easy to connect with (as I have been told by numerous people), and I think that is why people have been so touched by his message and interested to hear his reflections. My dad has since co-founded an organisation to tackle hate crime — I4GiveH8 — he has spoken to children across multiple schools about the power of forgiveness, and he has set an example for others about facing difficulty whilst upholding the best of principles. I can only hope that if I ever face adversity myself, I am able to deal with it in the same way I have seen my parents do so.

My dad once told me that as the details of our memories fade, the primary things we are left with are how we felt at those specific moments in time. So, whilst the details of this event have gradually become hazy for me, I am still left with the overwhelming feelings I experienced throughout, and they are feelings of immense gratitude and pride.

Oaiss Kurdy

The incident involving my father was devastating for the family. We have never dealt with an issue that has required such an exhausting amount of patience. I was told about the incident later on in the evening by my mother shortly after the attack had taken place. I cannot specifically remember where I was or what I was doing but I do remember that I rushed home to check on the family. I immediately called my father to make sure that he was aware that we knew, as a family, and to ask him if there was anything I could do for him. It is difficult to recall all the emotions I was feeling that day. However, knowing that my father was okay and hearing his voice on the phone gave me the strength to calm down and just be there, emotionally and physically for my family. I recall a lot of my friends, Muslim and non-Muslim, were extremely angered as they couldn't imagine anyone less deserving of an attack, especially one that was fuelled by hatred. My sister and I released a statement on Facebook regarding the attack with the aim of thanking people for their support and also reminding everyone to stay patient in times of difficulty, and, specifically, not to act irrationally as retaliation in any form.

I recall a lot of our friends visiting us and sitting with my mother and all this was difficult to watch. It was the first time we faced such an issue as a family, though I believe my dad's approach to the whole situation calmed everyone around him. It was this approach which had a knock-on effect by then inspiring many other people to follow suit with forgiveness.

Of the whole process, the court hearing was undoubtably the most difficult part to endure. Although forgiveness is a fundamental part of moving forward with these problems, justice is equally as important. As Muslims, we believe that justice will be brought to everyone and no sin will be unaccounted for. However, it is still a duty for the justice system to treat my dad with the respect and integrity that he deserved for having dealt with a near-death experience. It was my first time at a court hearing, and I was shocked by the process and outcome. I recall that our lawyer, the prosecutor, was very young, yet the public defender was experienced and of good age. I was only able to attend the last hearing, by which time the defendant had admitted to the intent of killing. Whilst watching the two lawyers, it was clear that the gap in competence was too high, which was painful to tolerate. The experienced defender was able to bend the clause of intent to psychological instability and the prosecutor was unable to convince the jury that the defendant had the intention to murder, even though the evidence was all in favour of the prosecutor, such as the attack, the weapon, the location and the statements.

I felt that the system was not fair in this regard. God forbid my father died in that attack, would the jury have had the same feelings, and would the prosecutor have done a better job in expressing my father's case? It is impossible to give a definite answer, yet it was all very frustrating to watch and endure. My dad later exited the courthouse knowing that someone tried to kill him but was fortunate enough to slither out of the "intent" aspect of the attack. That was painful to watch.

By the grace of God, our dad remains alive to guide us through our lives and we thank God for that blessing. Many people do not come out of a hate crime alive and forgiving. However, my dad was able to make the best out of an extremely dire situation. I think our feelings about the events are unanimous amongst my siblings and I feel very fortunate and proud to be raised under his roof.

Shahyda Chaudhry

I arrived at the centre on Grove Lane for a management committee meeting, and as I was running late, I rushed towards the back hall. I walked in, I noticed the table and chairs had been set up on the far wall, but the room was empty. A fellow committee member, Raheela Baloch, walked out the kitchen and she informed me that congregational prayer was being held in the other hall and that was where everyone was. She started to pray, and I sat down, checking my emails on my phone.

Suddenly, the door was flung open and as I looked up, Dr Nasser Kurdy came running in. He didn't say anything immediately and I remember thinking that was odd, why is he running, why has he got his shoes on (we always remove our shoes before entering the mosque)? He then ran over to the far wall and he picked up a chair, by now I was standing, and I called out "Dr Nasser, Dr Nasser, what are you doing?" He was running with the chair held up against his chest with the legs facing out, running back towards the door he had come in from. I ran towards him, calling his name, and then he stopped, looked at me and I think he said "I've been stabbed". I felt a chill come over me. I knew I had to get him to sit down and call for an ambulance. I looked over and saw that Raheela was still praying, so I shouted out for her to come and help.

I took the chair off Nasser and sat him down. I remember talking to him, asking where he had been struck, was he bleeding, etc. and I then rang 999. He was calm but very pale, with his head down, and he was worried about the perpetrator coming in. I think the shock of what was happening made me calm and I became focused on getting help. In the midst of all this I had forgotten that there were people in the other hall, but when I remembered, I left Nasser with Raheela and ran over to the other hall, where the door was now open, and people were putting on their shoes. I shouted out that Nasser had been attacked and we needed help. People rushed in behind me, and it became quite chaotic with lots of people in the hall asking Nasser questions. There was a doctor who helped press down on his wound. The police and paramedics arrived, and I felt a sense of relief that the professionals were here, and so Nasser would be OK.

When you are in the midst of an event like this it is hard to process what is happening in real time. The enormity of what happened occurred to me only after. At the time my main concern was making sure Dr Nasser survived and received medical help. I hadn't the time to ask questions about the who, the why, the how. What Ian Rooke did, did not just affect Nasser; it affected the whole community, and two years later the sense of fear attending mosque, and the prospect of being attacked for looking like a Muslim, these are still with us. We could no longer feel entirely safe after hate reached a small, quiet place called Hale.

Rabbi Amir Ellituv

As the Rabbi of the Sephardi congregation of Shaare Hayim that has a synagogue in Hale Barns, I have come to know Nasser Kurdy over the years, mainly through our meetings by the Cenotaph during Remembrance Sunday. When meeting Nasser, you automatically feel a special warmth and spiritual aura that he has around him; that made our connection even stronger.

I still recall seeing a headline pop up on my phone saying, "Religious Leader in Hale Barns Stabbed". At the time we never knew whether it was a hate crime, but regardless of that, I felt my heart sink and right away wrote a get-well letter and letter of support from our congregation. I sent Nasser a text message, and in the middle of the morning went to the Community Centre on Grove Lane and dropped off the letter. At the same time, there was a journalist from Radio Key 103 who asked me for my comment. I can't remember what I said but I felt that the blade that went into Nasser pierced all our hearts.

During the day we had a big event planned with our chief Rabbi coming to speak to our congregation, but throughout the day Nasser was on our minds, and then

Mother Claire Jacquiss rang me to say that there would be a vigil in the Grove Lane Community Centre, would I and my congregation be able to attend. I said certainly. Our Chief Rabbi spoke in our synagogue and then I asked our congregation to please join me in attending Grove Lane Community Centre to show solidarity with our friend Nasser Kurdy, and a large group came.

My Arabic isn't great, but what I do know very well are the swear words and curses! However, I knew that my plan was to start my speech in Arabic, sending love and greetings, which I did. The funny thing was I had to stop and change to English because the only other words I knew weren't appropriate! But I spoke and hope that I touched people's hearts.

The next day I received a most wonderful message from Nasser, and even though I don't have it I still remember clearly how he said, "Amir, you are the first person I am contacting, and I wish to share with you the special light from above, how miraculously the blade had missed my vital organs by millimetres." Nasser was so appreciative of the love and support that he had received.

As Nasser recovered, we wanted him to speak in our synagogue, which he did so eloquently, and following the service he ate in our home for Sabbath lunch. The connection that Nasser had with those around the table together who heard him speak was very special. One of our members had been treated by Nasser in the past as a patient, and they kept on telling us what a unique individual Nasser is. Nasser is a person who when you see him, after not seeing one another for many months, instantly you have a close connection with him as if you have never left each other. His smile, the heart that he wears so openly and warmly, the sincerity that he always shows, the care that he displays make Nasser who he is.

The person who attacked Nasser never realised that through his actions he had brought Nasser so much closer to our hearts. May Nasser be blessed together with his lovely family for years of joy, health and happiness Inshallah.

Haitham Nadeem

When we were visiting our family in late September, my wife received a phone call from a friend telling her that Dr Kurdy had been stabbed. All I could hear was my wife screaming. We left our children at my sister's house and went straight to the hospital, not knowing what happened, how it happened, if he was OK, etc. Our heads were consumed with thoughts, worry and fear. At the same time, we kept wondering as to why would anyone attack someone like Nasser, who is well known for being such a peaceful and highly respected person.

The journey to the hospital was achingly long. After finally arriving and seeing Dr Kurdy's wife and some of our friends, we were not allowed to go into the room to see him, but it was a huge relief when we were told that his condition was stable. We stayed until he was discharged and was taken by one of our friends back to his house.

At some point in our lives, almost inevitably, most of us will live through a terrifying event. It could be a car accident, a natural disaster, a medical emergency, a fire, or perhaps a trauma inflicted by another person in the form of assault, abuse or robbery. Trauma can also come from seeing another person be seriously hurt or even killed, or from learning about something awful that happened to a person we love. Whatever the source, trauma leaves its imprint on the brain. We knew Nasser was still alive, and fine, but it took us a long time to recover from this trauma. The shock was even bigger because it was Nasser Kurdy. He is such a lovely, peaceful, caring and kind person whom everyone loves. He is always keen to bring communities together and he is an active member of the AMA Interfaith group.

It made us feel unsafe and uncomfortable living here. We were not thinking about the perpetrator and we didn't feel any sense of anger or hatred towards him; all that was on our minds was Dr Kurdy's safety and the potential impact of such an act on our relationship as a Muslim community with other community groups in the area, which has always been that of mutual respect and friendship. We were incredibly inspired by Dr Kurdy's reaction to the event and his emphasis on forgiveness.

Saima Alvi

Brother Nasser Kurdy has been a family friend for many years, and I have worked with him as a colleague at Altrincham Mosque for the past 12 years now. I have always found Br Nasser to be a calm and collected type of person who is very personable and will always try and fight someone's cause if there is a need. On the evening of Sunday 24 September 2017 at around 17.30, we had a Mosque management meeting arranged. That afternoon, I happened to attend another important community meeting in Cheetham Hill (about 14 miles away from Altrincham). I had mentioned to the meeting lead that I needed to leave by 17:00 as it would take 30 mins to reach Altrincham. However, it seems that the Biriyani saved me. Superintendent Umer Khan produced a pan of Biriyani at 17:00 and said his sister had made it and we couldn't leave until we had eaten it. That was my saving grace as I left at around 17:25 and arrived at Altrincham Mosque at about 17:50. Unbeknown to me at the time, Br Nasser had been mercilessly stabbed in a knife attack as he entered Altrincham Mosque at around 17:40.

When I arrived, my heart missed a few beats as I saw lots of blue flashing lights, including at least three police cars and an ambulance. I scurried into the main hall of the Mosque and to my shock saw Br Nasser being attended to by paramedics who were assessing a neck injury and about to lay him down on a stretcher. I quickly gathered from two female friends that as Br Nasser entered the grounds a man tried to stab him in the neck and Br Nasser ran towards the main building. As he entered the main Mosque building, he realised that there were two women inside, and very bravely and valiantly Br Nasser picked up a chair and went towards the attacker who had pursued him. At this point the attacker retreated and ran back down the Mosque's footpath out onto the road.

I was mortified and scared. Were there more attackers? What was the motive? How could anyone attack our beautiful peaceful Mosque and even more worryingly how could anyone attack someone as kind-hearted and friendly as Br Nasser? All these questions raced through my mind.

However, working as a school lead, I am a practically minded person, and my training has taught me to respond to emergencies swiftly and calmly. I asked Br Nasser if his wife Syrsa was informed of the attack. Br Nasser replied, "No and please don't tell her — she'll be really worried." At that point I spoke to the Chair of the Mosque and said that Syrsa MUST be informed, despite Br Nasser's wish, and the Chair agreed. I drove the short distance of one mile to the Kurdys' residence, along with the Mosque Chair's wife, Shahnaz. Syrsa, who is also a good friend of mine, opened the door and I chose my words carefully and calmly, telling her that Br

Nasser was fine but there had been an incident at the Mosque, and I went on to tell her the story as I knew it at that point.

Syrsa, another practical person, looked a little pale but she was very calm. I said she should go to the hospital and I would drive her. She said that if it was a trouble, she would drive herself. I said absolutely not and that it was no trouble at all. I wanted to support her at this very difficult time.

On arrival at Wythenshawe Emergency Department, in the waiting room we met a Mosque committee member, Amjad, as he had accompanied Br Nasser in the ambulance. We were in the waiting room for at least three hours and to our surprise, very quickly, within about an hour we received a confirmed report that the police had detained and arrested a suspect who they believed was responsible for Br Nasser's attack. It transpired that the suspect's brother had come back to the crime scene—which I subsequently discovered is very common practice for criminals.

Br Nasser was being seen to by colleagues as he works as a Consultant Orthopaedic Surgeon in the same hospital. It was clear that his colleagues were horrified, and it took some time before Syrsa was able to visit. Several other friends turned up in the waiting room as the shocking news of the stabbing was spreading like wildfire around the community. He had suffered a wound to the left side of the back of his neck which was 5 cm deep. It was discovered that the wound had missed his jugular vein and spinal cord by millimetres, and he was lucky to get away with only stitches. After a few hours, amazingly and by the grace of God, Br Nasser was discharged, and characteristically he seemed in good spirits.

Late that Sunday evening, I was asked to attend Altrincham Police Station for a specially convened meeting with another member from Altrincham Mosque and the Assistant Chief Constable. Russ Jackson was a senior ranking officer and linked to the Counter Terrorism Unit. At this point the facts were vague and disjointed but with a Muslim being stabbed entering the Mosque, there was a possible terrorism link. Mr Jackson gave us some facts about what they knew at that stage such that they believed this was not a targeted attack, but more likely a random attack and it could have been anyone on that road. I wasn't so convinced.

For the next two or three days my sister Aisha and I were asked by Br Nasser and Syrsa to attend their residence as there were various journalists turning up for the scoop. This story was major and was covered by all the major networks including BBC, ITV, C4, national and local papers, including tabloids and broadsheets, as well as radio. We carefully checked who wanted interviews and informally managed the process in as orderly a way as we could. Br Nasser publicly declared "I have absolutely no anger or hate, or anything negative towards him. I have declared it; I have totally forgiven him. He could be a marginalised person within his own community." This was quite a unique stance from Br Nasser; however, it was also one that was not necessarily endorsed by all members of the Muslim community. Some felt the forgiveness stance weakened the position of Muslims in the UK and might not act as a deterrent against future hate-fuelled attacks. I discussed this with Br Nasser, but he did not agree with this point of view and he felt comfortable about forgiving his attacker.

In the first few days at the Kurdy residence, Br Nasser was surprisingly perky, but it seemed that the possible consequences of what could have happened to Br Nasser hit Syrsa. At one point, I recall she looked worried and I distinctly remember on a couple of occasions Br Nasser just sweetly giving her a reassuring hug.

Within two days, Br Nasser's dining table had filled up with cards arriving internationally, nationally and locally. There were so many messages of kindness from complete strangers in addition to many beautiful messages of love and concern from Nasser's adoring patients. Quotes included:

> I am just appalled by this terrible attack on this good man who spends his life helping others. I shall never understand the total ignorance of anyone who would do this while harbouring such hatred.

> An orthopaedic surgeon that has probably saved countless lives, attacked in this way, I'm sickened. My thoughts and prayers are with his family at this time.

The day following the stabbing on the Monday evening, an impromptu gathering was organised by Altrincham Mosque for "the much-loved and respected surgeon who had helped victims of the Manchester bombing." A 'peace and unity vigil' was attended by the Muslim community and people of all faiths as well as none. It was a heart-warming and emotional gathering which pulled together the community who were also in shock and were able to console each other. A few days after the attack Br Nasser asked me to accompany him to Altrincham Police Station where he gave a statement about the attack in the form of a video interview. This was an extremely stressful few days for Br Nasser, but he embraced the situation with grace and calmness.

The culprit's trial began in March 2018 and I attended for several days along with a couple of my family members to support Br Nasser and his family. At the trial, the culprit and his mother had apologised to Br Nasser who had reciprocated by having a civil conversation with the mother. The culprit was cleared by a jury of attempted murder but admitted wounding with intent and possession of an offensive weapon. In August 2018 he was sentenced to five years and four months in prison.

We are very grateful to the Almighty for saving Br Nasser and I always joke with him that the evening of his stabbing he was slightly late in attending the congregational prayer. I joke that in future don't be late for prayers or you never know what might happen!

Ripples: Nasser Kurdy

The following three sections are examples of some of the many written statements and speeches Dr Kurdy has given since the events of September 2017. The first is the text of the statement read out on Dr Kurdy's behalf at Ian Rooke's sentencing, while the others are from presentations Dr Kurdy has given at commemorative events.

Victim Impact Statement

I, Nasser Kurdy, am a Consultant Orthopaedic Surgeon at Wythenshawe Hospital. I have practiced as an Orthopaedic Consultant for over twenty years in Manchester. On 24 September 2017 at 17:40 I was stabbed in the back of the neck in an unprovoked attack on the grounds of Altrincham Islamic Cultural Centre in Hale. I make this statement to the best of my knowledge and believe this to be a true and accurate reflection of my experience of the attack.

Immediately after my stabbing, my medical knowledge allowed me to appreciate that no major harm took place. When I later saw my scans, it was only then that I knew how close I was to being killed. Only 2 cm separated the tip of the knife from my spinal cord. On the night of the stabbing, I asked my wife how she felt. Her words were: I feel the mercy of God has touched you. This has been and has always been the overwhelming appreciation of my stabbing. I could have easily died on the day but for the mercy and the grace of God. We are a family and a community guided by our faith. We are of the belief that nothing befalls us except what has been written for us and we also believe in the power of forgiveness. Through that, we have forgiven Ian for what he did, and we have no animosity or resentment towards him or towards his family.

The victim impact statement is invariably about the adverse impact a crime may have had on the victim. The truth in my case is that apart from a temporary period of excruciating pain and ongoing mild discomfort in my neck, the physical impact has been no more than that. The psychological impact was also short lived. I was able to overcome my fears within a short period of time and was back to my normal self very soon after the stabbing. From a financial point of view, my work was not affected as I was back to work within two days and was back to full capacity within a week. My family did not suffer either. I was stabbed on Sunday evening and my son was back to school the following morning. My wife drove him to school at half past eight as usual. My older son and my daughter were also relatively unaffected. My community, on the other hand, were probably the most affected. The stabbing took place on the grounds of my local Islamic centre and considering the recent rise of far-right activity locally, this probably caused the biggest concern. As the vice chair of my centre, I am grateful for the visible police presence for the two weeks after my stabbing. This helped restore calm and normality to my community.

This however is not the full story. Since my stabbing, I have suffered from what is better known as post-traumatic growth syndrome. The stabbing has had an unbelievable positive impact on me. I am a much better person for having gone through this ordeal. This has been partly due to my faith, partly due to my family but mostly due to the people around me. I cannot thank enough my community, the public, my colleagues at work, my patients and people that I may never meet for their expression of love and support towards me and towards my family. I can never put into words the generosity of such a response which even up till now still continues. I am a much happier man than before. My outlook on life has changed to the better. I have met many wonderful people and I have new purposes in my life. I feel that my forgiveness has touched many people positively. I was told that at one of my local schools where the children were being taught about forgiveness, I was the example that was given to them. Many people tell me to my face how good they felt about what I did. I cannot put into words how immensely rewarding this was for me.

I can go on much more about the positive impact of knowing just how close I came to dying and how miraculously the path of the knife missed everything vital in my neck. Only I as a surgeon will ever know that. As a man of faith, it is inevitable that I will attribute such a miracle to Almighty God. My stabbing has placed me even closer to God and in some weird way I have also accepted my fate of dying one day. The thoughts of dying no longer trouble me.

Everyone knows that I publicly forgave Ian on Monday morning for what he did to me the previous day. My stance on forgiveness and on countering hate narratives has also been a significant positive turn in my life. I have cofounded the organisation I4giveH8. My stabbing has paved the way for me to be involved in countering hate and helping others understand the power of forgiveness. This is something that I would have never done if it wasn't for being stabbed. This brings me to my final point. When I look at Ian, my heart only feels sadness and compassion. Sadness for how such a young person can end up doing what he did and compassion in wanting to help him to better himself. For some reason I have been unable to hate him. What he did to me was very serious and I know that the judicial system will run its course. But for me, there can only be justice if Ian becomes a better person and I hope that I am permitted to be part of his rehabilitation.

Birmingham Holocaust Memorial Day 2020

We have listened to a great deal of pain this evening where humans dive into the abyss of inhumanity. All I can do this evening is share with you a message of hope. Let me first share with you a WhatsApp post that was circulated in my locality in South Manchester shortly after the 19 June 2017 attack on Finsbury Park Mosque:

> I watched that van plough into those people at Finsbury Park Mosque and thought OMG that could have been me. Then I remembered, I didn't have a white van.

Let me introduce myself: I am Dr Nasser Kurdy, I am a senior Orthopaedic Surgeon at South Manchester, I am also an Imam at my local mosque in Hale. I am married with three children. As a Manchester based orthopaedic surgeon, I was privileged to have treated victims of the Manchester Arena bombing.

At the age of 58 and for my sins I was stabbed in the back of my neck in an unprovoked attack on the grounds of my local mosque in Altrincham on 24 September 2017. A young man, Ian, sneaked up behind me and with a lashing move plunged his knife into the back of my neck. By the grace of only 2 cm, I lived to tell the tale. He proceeded to run after me, but somehow, my 58-year-old legs were just too good on the day. It goes without saying that I am very happy to be alive and very privileged to be addressing you on this Memorial Day.

The first point I want to share with you this evening is the propensity for such a violent act to promote the hate narrative on both sides, the Islamist and the far right. Such hateful people are always ready to jump on the bandwagon to propel their hateful narrative. The fact that I publicly forgave my attacker so early, silenced the hate narrative completely. Even though my story was aired internationally, no one could raise the hate narrative. No one was able to use my story to stir up hate. My story was all about forgiveness. It was then that I learned that forgiveness is just as infectious as hate, but much more powerful.

The second point I want to share with you is that just as much as we have backstage racists who are ready to jump on the bandwagon and thrash about their vile comments, we have many more silent people that are moved by forgiveness.

Following my stabbing, I received over 3000 messages (emails, texts, WhatsApp) and over 400 cards, with the cards being mostly from strangers. One such card from a total stranger from London read: I don't know you, but the act of forgiveness has inspired me. I am donating on your behalf to "Islamic Relief". This was just one example.

As I said, the power of forgiveness is infectious principally because it delivers hope. It is vitally important to work and develop the narrative of forgiveness and of hope.

The third point is that the honest truth, and the interesting thing that happened to me was the fact that I was unable to hate the person who stabbed me. It is probably a combination of my faith and my profession and the fact that I have a wonderful and supportive family and community. My inability to hate that young man had a profound impact on me. Just as much as there is a spiral that takes us from hate to violence, there is another spiral that takes us from forgiveness to compassion. You can't just forgive and do nothing.

Not being able to hate actually made me feel sympathetic towards the young man who stabbed me. As we look at our attackers, we come to realise that even though what they did was monstrous, they are invariably pathetic people. Ian was a petty thief. Unemployed. Has mental-health issues. His father is an alcoholic. I said very early that the crime committed against me was years in the making and he was not the only guilty party. Many systems that exist to safeguard this young man have failed him. In their failure, they have also failed me.

However, the act of forgiveness has set me on a path that I did not expect or plan. I now address our future generation with the message that forgiveness has amazing powers, but it takes a leap of faith and a bigger leap of strength. I do not know where to take this message from here, but I feel that there is more to be done to harness this powerful and this positive message.

Can I finish by saying that I am very grateful for the community coordinators' support in keeping me going despite my demanding work schedule. If there is one last message to give you here today it is to maintain the support and funding for the work on promoting community cohesion and promoting events such as today's where we painfully remember and commemorate so that we say again "never again".

Knife-Crime Vigil, Manchester Cathedral 2019

I would like to share with you a few thoughts.

Thank you for giving me the privilege of this platform. Sadly, I earned this privilege as I was the victim of a knife crime.

My name is Dr Nasser Kurdy, I was stabbed in the back of my neck over two years ago by a complete stranger. The Almighty has given me a new lease of life and I promised that I was not going to be complacent anymore.

My contribution to this evening is very personal to me so please forgive me if I offend anyone here. I hope you find my contribution useful.

The first thought I would like to share with you is this: the moment Ian Rourke stabbed me, his life changed. The moment I forgave him my life changed. Ian is now in prison. But I set off on a journey based on forgiveness. Yesterday I was at Thorn Cross prison participating in the Sycamore restorative programme for the prisoners. And this morning I was addressing school children in Rotherham tackling the harms of hate. I was able to do so, I was able to engage positively because I forgave my attacker. I can never over emphasize the power of forgiveness to heal.

My second thought follows on from this and it is a plea to the victims and the loved ones of victims who are struggling to forgive. I know that I have no right to say that, but in the book *Why Forgive?* Steven McDonald summed it up for me. He was a NY police officer who was shot in the spine and was paralysed from the neck downwards. He said that he only started to heal when he was able to forgive. It is very difficult, very, very difficult to forgive, but not forgiving is even more difficult.

The third thought is painful and difficult. Victims of knife crime and their loved ones suffer twice. Having suffered the trauma of the crime, victims and their families have to endure the judicial process. To some, this can be just as traumatic as the crime itself, if not more so. We need to appreciate that the judicial process is underpinned by fairness to the accused. This is very, very painful for the victims and their loved ones. Having been through such a process, I fully support and endorse the fairness to the accused. But the victims of knife crime and their loved ones need to be empowered and need to be part of that process and need a voice. A victim impact statement at the end of the proceedings is not a voice. This issue has to be addressed.

But now to my main point. I want to introduce you to the young man who nearly killed me. His name is Ian Rourke. His dad is suffering from alcohol related illness. His mum tries her best to make ends meet. His granddad suffers from chronic lung disease and has been in and out of hospital. Ian has a criminal record. He suffers from mental-health problems and is on medication. As a doctor and by any of the measures I know, he is a vulnerable adult. On the day he stabbed me, he literally went "mental", picked up a knife and headed out to kill someone, anyone. The crime committed against me was instigated many years before that fateful moment. Ian is not the only one guilty of my stabbing.

In addition to all the inspirational talks we have had the privilege to listen to this evening, my humble contribution for tonight is this, and I think I echo some of what was said earlier: "one of the issues we need to address is the vulnerability of those committing knife crime". This is something that is very relevant to my crime.

I would sincerely want to leave you with my last thought, and it is from the heart. Forgiving is not about condoning the action, but it is about healing, moving and contributing.